101 Tips
for You
and Your Home

★101★

Tips for You and Your Home

★

The Editors of Consumer Reports Books

★

Consumers Union
Mount Vernon, New York

Our special thanks to Walter Leonard

Copyright © 1989 by Consumers Union of U.S., Inc.,
Mount Vernon, New York 10553
All rights reserved, including the right of reproduction
in whole or in part in any form.
ISBN: 0-89043-299-6
Design by Victoria Hartman
First printing, February 1989
Manufactured in the United States of America

101 Tips for You and Your Home is a Consumer Reports Book
published by Consumers Union, the nonprofit organization that
publishes *Consumer Reports,* the monthly magazine of test reports,
product Ratings, and buying guidance. Established in 1936,
Consumers Union is chartered under the Not-For-Profit
Corporation Law of the State of New York.

The purposes of Consumers Union, as stated in its charter, are
to provide consumers with information and counsel on consumer
goods and services, to give information on all matters relating to
the expenditure of the family income, and to initiate and to
cooperate with individual and group efforts seeking to create and
maintain decent living standards.

Consumers Union derives its income solely from the sale of
Consumer Reports and other publications. In addition, expenses of
occasional public service efforts may be met, in part, by
nonrestrictive, noncommercial contributions, grants, and fees.
Consumers Union accepts no advertising or product samples and
is not beholden in any way to any commercial interest. Its
Ratings and reports are solely for the use of the readers of its
publications. Neither the Ratings nor the reports nor any
Consumers Union publications, including this book, may be used
in advertising or for any commercial purpose. Consumers Union
will take all steps open to it to prevent such uses of its materials,
its name, or the name of *Consumer Reports.*

Contents

3 ■ PROTECTING YOUR POCKETBOOK

4 ■ MAKING THE MOST OF YOUR LEISURE

5 ■ KEEPING HEALTHY

6 ▪ FOOD AND NUTRITION

7 ▪ WISDOM IN THE KITCHEN

8 ▪ KEEPING WARM, KEEPING COOL

9 ∎ CAREFREE WASHDAYS

Introduction

101 Tips for You and Your Home is a mixture of useful facts, important information, and practical advice to help you with the day-to-day running of your home, the daily maintenance of your health, and the safe use of your leisure time. It can help you shop for an air conditioner, decide whether you want to make your own videos, or find the right life insurance policy. You'll get tips on using your appliances efficiently, advice on taking the best snapshots, the facts on insomnia. It answers your questions on many facets of home maintenance, too: What's the best paint to use on exterior siding? Should I change my oil furnace to gas? What should I look for in a refrigerator? With this book, you will also find out how to care for a lot of household items—and save money and time in the process.

Consumer Reports is the source of all the information found here. In these few pages we have condensed many of the most popular articles that appeared in the magazine over the past few years. We don't go into any topic in depth; for a complete report on the subject, we refer you to the magazine. But *101 Tips* does give you the most important facts about a product or service—quickly, concisely, and accurately.

101 Tips for You and Your Home is easy to use. Simply refer to the table of contents, where each topic is listed alphabetically under a main subject heading.

We hope you will find these tips informative, stimulating, and fun to read.

The Editors of Consumer Reports Books

★ 1 ★

Around the House

BATHROOM CLEANERS

Many bathroom-cleaning products claim to kill germs. That's a meaningless claim, even if true. There's no point to killing germs unselectively in an unsterile room—new bacteria promptly replace the dead ones.

Another typical claim for bathroom cleaners is based on antimildew ingredients. However, straight chlorine bleach is a much more effective mold fighter, though it isn't a good all-around cleaner. That being so, you may be tempted to make your own bathroom cleaner by mixing bleach with other cleaning products. Don't. Bleach reacts almost instantly with acid to produce hazardous chlorine gas, and with ammonia and related alkaline substances to produce a mix of chlorine and other noxious gases.

That's not to say you shouldn't use bleach in a room regularly scrubbed down with a cleaner. Just use the two separately. Rinse surfaces washed with bleach thoroughly—a good idea anyway, since unwiped bleach is apt to mar smooth surfaces. Bleach residues that soak into tile grout will help prevent mold from taking hold again, but won't be present in amounts that can hurt you the next time you use another cleaner.

CARPETS

Some things to do *before* you shop for a wall-to-wall carpet:

Decide on color. Very light or very dark colors show dirt more than medium tones do; solids show dirt more than multiple tones.

Gather swatches and paint chips to take with you, in case the store won't let you take sample pieces of carpet home. Try to look at carpet samples in the same kind of light you have at home.

The carpet you get may vary somewhat from the store sample. If you want to match a shade precisely, try to work from the actual carpet roll.

Measure the area to be carpeted. For an idea of the square yardage you'll need, divide your square footage by nine. That figure can serve as a multiplier when you consider square-yard prices.

The store will send someone to your home to measure more precisely. The yardage you are quoted is apt to be higher than the yardage you calculated. Most carpeting is 12 feet wide and must be pieced out or cut down when installed. Closets and doorways can also add yardage, as do allowances for matching a pattern or pile direction.

Ask to see the installer's plan—so you know where seams will be located. By living with one more seam in a room, you may be able to buy less carpet.

Consider traffic patterns. For better performance, match the carpet to its use.

• *Kitchen and bathroom.* A synthetic face fiber and a fully synthetic backing will resist moisture and mildew. Polypropylene resists water-based stains, so it's a good choice. Use a thin, dense foam-rubber or urethane pad underneath. A kitchen carpet should also have a low, very dense pile that will keep crumbs on top so they can be vacuumed up. In the bathroom, consider a washable carpet that you can cut and fit yourself.

• *Living room.* Smooth plushes or Saxonies look luxurious and formal, but they show footprints—especially in light, bright colors. If the room gets a lot of use, check the recommendations below for dining and family rooms.

• *Dining and family rooms.* The latest nylon carpets, with built-in stain resistance, are good bets for well-traveled areas where food may be spilled. Light colors show stains and wear. Textured constructions such as frieze or cut-and-loop help hide signs of use; level-loop or low-cut pile is easiest to vacuum. A dense hair-and-jute pad underneath will help the carpet wear well.

• *Bedrooms.* Carpets of almost any construction will do where there's little traffic. Here you can indulge in light colors, deep pile, and thick padding. A carpet that feels soft to the hand will be appreciated in an area where you often go barefoot. Conversely, if you have to scrimp, it will matter least here.

• *Stairs and halls.* For high-traffic areas, low level-loop or low, dense, cut-pile carpets give the best wear. Deep pile on stairs won't wear as well, and it can be slippery. Medium solid colors or multicolors such as tweeds or Berbers show dirt least. Use firm underpadding such as felted hair-and-jute, a double layer on stairs. Foam rubber and urethane pads can be too bouncy for safety on stairs.

Once you've settled on a carpet, ask exactly what the total price includes. Find out if you have to pay extra for moving furniture, removing door saddles and floor moldings, and disposing of the old carpet and padding. Stairs and other tricky installations will probably entail an extra charge.

Your written agreement with the store should include your carpet's precise name and color, the total square yards, such installation details as the location of seams, and the installation date.

DRAIN CLEANING

What's the best way to keep your drains flowing? Pour some boiling water down them about once a week. Pour in half a gallon, wait a few minutes, then pour in another half gallon. Boiling water may crack porcelain fixtures, so pour directly into the drain rather than into the basin.

If a drain nonetheless becomes clogged, avoid chemical drain cleaners, which are among the most hazardous of consumer products. Strongly corrosive, they open a blocked drain by eating and boiling their way through the clog. Such strong chemicals can severely damage your eyes, lungs, and skin. Accidentally swallowing even a small amount can cause injury or death. It is far safer and no less effective to use a mechanical device.

Try a rubber plunger first. It's cheap, easy to use, and usually works. Alternatively, try a product that uses pressurized air or gas to push an obstruction past the bend in the drainpipe. But beware of the pressure if you have old, corroded drain lines.

Stubborn clogs call for the service of a licensed plumber, lest you damage yourself or the plumbing.

FABRIC PILL REMOVERS

Pilling, that unsightly accumulation of fuzz balls, generally occurs when fibers are worked loose from a fabric by rubbing. The resulting ''pills'' are held in place by fibers that still hold firm. Loosely woven and knitted synthetics and blends are especially apt to pill, but woolens aren't immune. Pills can form on clothes, blankets, and upholstery fabrics, but sweaters seem especially vulnerable.

Some new gadgets to remove pills include several little electric shavers run by a dry-cell battery. A fan-shaped blade sweeps behind a screen with holes large enough for most pills to poke through. The shavers' effectiveness depends mostly on the fabric and the density of the pilling. Shavers work best on small pills, especially those on unnapped fabrics.

Another kind of gadget is the snagger, with rough surfaces that snag pills and rip them off. A snagger works best on large pills, especially those on firmly constructed materials such as overcoating or heavy weaves. They can also restore a fabric's nap.

Shavers work better than snaggers on stretchy knits, which tend to be pulled and distorted by a snagger. If you have sweaters with light pilling and an overcoat with heavy pilling, you need both a shaver and a snagger.

Still another way to remove pills is with a common safety razor, shaving the pilled area as one would shave skin. But extreme care is needed to avoid slitting fabrics and/or cutting yourself.

FIRE EXTINGUISHERS

Can you tell—in advance—how well a fire extinguisher will work? Yes, indeed. Extinguishers typically carry an Underwriters Laboratories (UL) rating. A reliable guide to performance, the rating is a set of numbers and letters that tell you what type and size of fire a unit can handle.

Extinguishers rated *1A* can put out a blazing test stack of 50 pieces of 20-inch-long wood 2 $\times$ 2's; *2A* models can put out a fire twice that size. *1B* models can extinguish $3\frac{1}{4}$ gallons of liquid fuel burning in a $2\frac{1}{2}$-square-foot pan. *C*-rated units (that letter is never preceded by a number) are safe for fires involving electrically live devices.

"All-purpose" (or "multipurpose") extinguishers use ammonium phosphate. They are effective against wood, fuel, and electrical fires. But despite that versatility, they aren't necessarily the best choice. For kitchen grease fires, an extinguisher that uses sodium bicarbonate will smother burning grease much faster and more thoroughly.

Ammonium phosphate and sodium bicarbonate both leave behind a messy, corrosive residue, not a material you'd want left on hi-fi equipment or a computer. Halon extinguishers are tidier. Those use halon gases, which leave no messy residue, to choke off a fire. Halon is also suitable for a class-C electrical fire, as well as class-B fires. Larger models work on class-A fires as well.

Conveniences. Look carefully at the following features:

- *Mounting.* Heavier models hang from a wall-mounted hook. Lighter units are strapped to a plate that's screwed to the wall. A few are held in place with a Velcro strip, but the strip's adhesive backing isn't likely to hold very well, except on a very smooth surface.

A mounting bracket should hold its extinguisher securely, but release it easily.

- *Pressure indicator.* A fire extinguisher may go unused for years; check its pressurization monthly. The best indicator is a dial-and-pointer gauge, which tells you the pressure at a glance. On some units, you push a plastic pin; if the pin pops back up, pressure is adequate.

Some halon models lack a pressure indicator—you check pressure by weighing the unit. That's a drawback; the weight must be precise to a fraction of an ounce, which is a precision beyond most household scales.

- *Temper seal.* A seal to prevent accidental firing should be easy to remove, to save precious fire-fighting time.

- *Firing mechanism.* You squeeze a pair of levers to fire most large dry-chemical models. Those models won't suit you unless you have a very firm grip.

- *Instructions.* An extinguisher should be marked

with easy-to-read words and pictures that show at a glance the steps to follow.

Every home should have a sodium-bicarbonate extinguisher in the kitchen, where most home fires begin. Buy an all-purpose extinguisher for the garage, the workshop, and other areas. It's a good idea to keep one under the driver's seat of a car.

Think of halon models as auxiliary extinguishers. Residue-free, they are unequaled for protecting prized objects. But they're expensive and usually too small to be the only fire protection in a garage or workshop.

Dry-chemical models are not only cheaper to buy but cheaper also to recharge. Still, recharging costs almost as much as a new fire extinguisher, especially for a small model. It makes sense to replace a small unit if its pressure drops too much or if it's been used.

GLUE

Most glues aren't jacks-of-all-trades. For successful repairs, you need to know their special talents:

Epoxy adhesives come in two parts, a resin and a hardener. These glues are hard, water-resistant, and very strong, with fine gap-filling abilities.

Catalyzed acrylic glues are strong, stick to oil surfaces, and can glue almost any material except flexible plastic.

Silicone rubber glues are not especially strong, but they take a very wide range of temperatures and are usable on most surfaces. Their elasticity, water-resistance, and gap-filling properties let them serve as sealants and caulks as well as adhesives. They can't be painted.

Cyanoacrylates, the "instant" glues, are fast-setting, although they have been reformulated to slow down their bonding speed to a manageable minute or so. Their quick bonding lets you glue hard-to-clamp objects. They don't fill gaps, so they're best for tight-fitting joints.

Contact cements are flexible adhesives used most often for gluing a plastic laminate to a countertop, resetting a loose wall tile, or reattaching a shoe sole. You put the glue on both surfaces to be joined and let it dry a bit. The glue then bonds the instant the surfaces are brought together. They can't be used for gluing joints that must be slid together for final assembly.

Plastic cements are clear adhesives in small squeeze tubes. They shrink as they dry, so they don't work well in loose joints. They're strong on wood, less strong on metal.

White glues are inexpensive, water-based, strong, paintable, and not very flexible. They take a while to harden and can be cleaned up with water before they set.

Aliphatics, also called ''carpenter's glues,'' grab faster than white glues, so they require a shorter clamping time. They also shrink less than white glues. Both white glues and aliphatics are mainly for wood and other porous materials.

Resin glues, because of their water-resistance, are often used in construction or marine applications. They are toxic and irritating. Although inconvenient to use, resin glues clasp wood powerfully and resist water well.

You should be able to handle most repairs and do-it-yourself projects with an epoxy glue for very strong bonds on a variety of materials, a white glue or an aliphatic for ease of use and strength on wood, and a cyanoacrylate for quick bonding of hard-to-mend items.

HOUSE PAINTS AND STAINS

For the outside of a house, latex paint is simpler to use than oil-based paint. It's easy to apply and adheres well to damp surfaces. It dries quickly. Spills and spatters as well as tools and hands clean up with plain water.

Oil-based (alkyd) paint dries faster than it used to—you could probably apply two coats in that many days. But you can't apply an alkyd paint to a damp surface, and you need solvent for cleanup.

Paint isn't your only option for sprucing up a home's exterior. Stain offers a mellow, weathered look that may be appropriate on some surfaces, for some styles of house, and in certain settings.

Stain is meant to soak into wood, leaving at most a very thin film on the surface. The texture of the wood shows through the color, an advantage if you like the effect.

Like paint, stain comes in water- and oil-based formulations. Oil-based stain outsells latex. Stain also comes in transparent, semitransparent, and opaque varieties.

Paint versus stain. Many manufacturers advise against using a stain over a painted or otherwise sealed surface. If a stain can't soak into wood, it may be more difficult to apply, may not cover well, and may fail prematurely.

Latex versus oil. Despite the convenience of latex, don't rule out oil-based paint and stain. Consider the surface you intend to cover. An alkyd product can be the best solution to common problems—peeling and flaking paint, for instance. Many homeowners say that their paint seems to peel when latex paint has been used over alkyd, or vice versa. Solution: Don't switch formulations; paint latex over latex, alkyd over alkyd.

Figuring your paint needs. Estimate the distance in feet from the top of the foundation to the eaves (add two feet if the roof is pitched). Now measure the distance around the foundation. Multiply the two numbers and divide the answer by the coverage on the paint can's label. That's how many gallons your house will need for one coat. You'll need only about half as much for a second coat. Be sure that all the cans you buy for the job have the same batch number.

Tools. A roller will speed up the job on flat surfaces. But only a brush will get under the bottom edge of lapped siding and shingles or work the paint into the textured surface of rough-cut shingles. With water-based paints and stains, use a brush with synthetic bristles.

Cleaning. Rent a power washer to save labor in removing eroding or peeling paint or stain, and to clean off dirt and grime.

Black speckles on the north side of a house could be dirt. They could be mildew, too. Don't paint or apply stain over mildew; it will pop right through the new surface. Test by spot-cleaning a section with a 50-50 solution of chlorine bleach and water. Mildew will discolor and disappear in minutes.

Surface preparation. Alligatored, checked, blistered, or wrinkled surfaces have to be scraped, wirebrushed, steel-wooled, or sandpapered. Paint won't hide such blemishes.

Repair or replace broken shingles or deteriorated siding. Replace dry, cracked caulk around windows and doors. Use wood filler or putty to cover nails that can rust. Apply sealer over knot holes and pitch streaks in new wood. Prime those areas as well as any bare wood.

LAWN MOWERS

In shopping for a lawn mower, you have important decisions to make: Should the mower be powered by gasoline, electricity, or muscle power? Should it be a push-it-yourself, self-propelled, or riding model?

Gasoline rotary mower. Most people choose a gasoline model for its power and mobility. Some have a two-cycle engine, which uses a mixture of gasoline and oil for both fuel and lubricant. But most have a more convenient four-cycle engine, which runs on straight gasoline and has a separate oil reservoir.

Gasoline mowers can be hard to start, but that's often because of an awkwardly placed starter cord that takes an inordinate effort to pull. *Any* gasoline mower can become hard to start if it isn't serviced and in tune. Gasoline mowers are also noisy enough to be a nuisance, though probably not enough to damage your hearing.

A gasoline-powered rotary lawn mower is also the kind to buy for a medium-sized lawn that's fairly flat and lacking in hard-to-mow areas. For a larger lawn, consider a self-propelled, gasoline-powered unit. Mowers with an engine that keeps running when you stop the blade are best for convenience.

If you usually bag clippings, a rear-bagger is your best bet—it holds more clippings than a mower whose bag protrudes to one side, and it lets you cut close to obstructions on either side of the mower. But if you don't use a grass bag, a side-discharge mower generally disperses clippings better than a rear-bagger does. With a side-discharge mower, however, you can't cut close to trees or flower beds from the right side—the discharge chute interferes.

Most side-discharge mowers, furthermore, offer a major inconvenience. They include a type of safety control that turns the engine off whenever you let go of the handle. You can buy an electric starter for some models, but that adds $50 to $100 to the price.

Electric rotary. Electric mowers are light, quiet, and easy to start, but their cord makes them awkward to use. Since they go only as far as their cord, they are limited to small lawns. (Mowing more than about a quarter of an acre requires too much cord to manage easily.) At that, an electric mower may make you cope with 100 feet or more of cord snaked across the lawn.

To deal with the electric-cord problem, you can coil the cord and mow back and forth, moving farther from the coil with each pass. Some mowers automatically keep the cord out of the way through a turn.

Riding mower. These machines cut a swath two to four feet wide. They're for homeowners with more than half an acre of lawn. The biggest models are small tractors that can be outfitted with attachments that plow snow, spread seed, and the like.

The odds of being injured with a riding mower are higher than with a walk-behind model. All new riding mowers have some important safety features—an interlock that prevents the engine from starting when the mower is in gear or the blade is engaged, a blade that stops quickly when you disengage it, and a "deadman" control that stops the blade automatically if you fall off or climb off the seat.

Reel mower. For very small lawns, you may want to consider a hand-powered reel mower. Reel mowers are small, lightweight, and very quiet. However, they can't handle grass or weeds more than three or four inches tall, and they can't trim as close to a fence or a wall as most rotary models. If you set a reel to cut grass short (good for low-growing grasses such as bermuda and bentgrass) you run the risk of scalping the lawn, particularly on rough, uneven ground.

RADON

Up to 20,000 Americans, it's estimated, will die this year from exposure to by-products of a colorless, odorless gas called radon. Formed from uranium, the gas is present almost everywhere and can easily seep into houses. Inhaling it or its decay products introduces radioactivity directly into the body. Only cigarette smoking is a surer road to lung cancer.

Happily, radon problems are easy to detect and, usually, to solve. Cheap ($10) activated-charcoal detectors can take radon readings in your basement in three to seven days. Mail the detector to a lab and you should have results in a week or two. Your state radiological-health agency can give you the address of a qualified laboratory.

Radon is measured in picocuries per liter of air. (A picocurie is a trillionth of a curie, a unit of radiation.) If your lab results are 5 picocuries or less, your risk is fairly low. Readings of 20 picocuries and up, however, indicate an urgent need for action.

Between 5 and 20 picocuries, correction is called for, but not urgently—it's wise to do a follow-up test. An alpha-track detector ($25 to $50) can be exposed in your family's living space for several months, then mailed to a lab. The results give a direct measure of your long-term average radon exposure.

Correcting a radon problem can be as simple as opening windows in your basement, installing a fan there, or caulking off the entry points of gas. Heavy contamination may call for elaborate venting systems costing as much as $2,000 to install. For a fuller discussion of your options, consult the booklet of the U.S. Environmental Protection Agency (EPA), "Radon Reduction Methods: A Homeowner's Guide," OPA-86-005. It's available through state radiological health programs.

For even more detail, consult EPA's "Radon Reduction Techniques for Detached Houses, Technical Guidance," EPA/625/5-86/019. Aimed at contractors, the publication is available from the Center for Environmental Research Information, Distribution, 26 W. St. Clair, Cincinnati, OH 45268. A thorough discussion of radon's risks, along with medical background and solutions, can be found in *Radon: A Homeowner's Guide to Detection and Control.* This book is available in bookstores or by mail for $10 plus $3 postage from Consumer Reports Books, 540 Barnum Ave., Bridgeport, CT 06608.

SPACKLING COMPOUNDS

Have you had difficulty getting nice, smooth patches in old walls? New, lightweight products make it easier to get good results. The newest spackling compounds are full of air, in tiny glass spheres that provide attractive new properties. In particular, they don't sag when you fill larger holes and gouges, and they're easy to use.

The lightweights compete mainly with two older formulations: Powdered compounds contain plaster of paris and other fillers; they have to be mixed carefully with water. Premixed, latex-based compounds are ready for immediate application.

For very large holes, or areas subject to wear and tear (around wall switches, for example), you may want something tougher than a lightweight compound. You're then best off with a powdered compound. Powders also do well in deep fills, and most are so hard that you may bend a nail hammered into the patch. (Try drilling a pilot hole first.)

Powdered products store well, if kept in a dry place. Puttylike premixed compounds may tend to dry out and harden once their containers have been opened.

Spackling alternatives. Wallboard compound, also known as tape-joint compound or joint cement, can serve for small spackling chores such as refilling hairline cracks. But the material is not an all-purpose patcher.

Plaster of paris can make a hard, quick-drying patch, but it doesn't offer any real advantage over an ordinary spackling compound. A surface to be patched must first be wet with water.

Patching plaster, like plaster of paris, is a gypsum product, but it has retarders to slow up drying. Patching plaster should take about 90 minutes to set, enough time to let you correct irregularities.

Homemade compounds such as flour and water, or even oatmeal, were usable when all paints were oil-based. They still can be, in a pinch, if you use an alkyd (oil) paint over them. They won't be satisfactory under latex paints.

TELEPHONES

Shopping for a telephone should be a hands-on experience. At a minimum, a store should let you work a phone's controls, hear its ring, and listen to voice quality on a call. Some retailers have "central office simulators," devices to put a phone through its paces. Others may even be unwilling to ring a phone for a customer. If that's the case, shop somewhere else. Here are some things to check:

The phone should feel comfortable to hold and to dial. You may prefer a traditional handset—the familiar bowed receiver, narrow in the middle and flared at the ends—a shape that's comfortable when you want to prop the receiver between head and shoulder for hands-free talking. The handset's disconnect button shouldn't be too close to chin level, lest you cut yourself off accidentally as you talk.

Some keyboards are too cramped to use easily. And some phones have only numbered keys—they lack the familiar letters. That may not seem important until you try dialing a number that combines letters and numbers.

Cordless telephones. A cordless phone won't deliver the voice quality you may be accustomed to, its background noise can be intrusive, and the batteries can be finicky or quit unexpectedly. Most cordless phones won't operate at all in a power blackout. With some cordless phones, strangers can eavesdrop. And a cordless phone is expensive—even at discount, two to three times as much as a good corded phone. Repairs are apt to be time-consuming and expensive.

Still, cordless phones are handy. They can be a boon for people with big houses and a benefit for the infirm. The phones also serve as portable extensions for rooms without telephone wiring.

VACUUM CLEANERS

Vacuum cleaners aren't interchangeable. The kind to buy depends on the jobs you want to do:

Uprights. An upright vacuum cleaner does the best job on carpets. Its power-driven, rotating beater/brush does most of the work; the suction serves mainly to blow the dirt into a filter bag on the handle. However, upright models aren't very useful for bare floors, and they're awkward in tight places. An upright can often be fitted with hoses and attachments to handle crevices and under-sofa or above-floor chores, but the arrangement is apt to be clumsy.

Canisters. A canister vacuum, with its higher suction, does the jobs an upright can't do well—bare floors, dusting, and the like. A canister is generally easy to use with attachments. However, an ordinary canister won't clean rugs as well as an upright. The canister relies on suction alone for cleaning; it picks up only surface dirt and debris, not deep-down grit.

Power-nozzle canisters. A canister with a

power-nozzle attachment combines an upright's deep-cleaning ability with a canister's convenience and versatility. Unfortunately, it also retains some of the canister's drawbacks. Some assembly is always required, as is a good tug on the hose every now and then to keep the canister trailing along behind you.

Compact canisters. You can generally carry a small version of a full-sized canister in one hand while you clean with the other. Compacts are good in places where you can't take a full-sized machine—the stairs or your car, for example. Some models have a power nozzle.

Lightweight uprights. These look a bit like a regular upright cleaner, but they lack a powered beater-brush. They're easy to handle and quite useful for quick cleanups of surface debris on carpets or bare floors.

You and Your Car

BUYING A USED CAR

Performance cars, luxury models, and convertibles are expensive even when secondhand, and many are packed with trouble-prone options. Your dollar will generally go further when you purchase a small or medium-size sedan.

If you can, buy a used car with a known history—from a trusted relative, friend, or neighbor. Be more wary with other private sellers. Ask about the car's condition and mileage, and ask to see repair bills. (At a minimum, check the service sticker on the doorjamb to see if the car has been regularly serviced.) Find out if the car has ever been in an accident. Ask why it's being sold; the seller may divulge a problem you'd rather not cope with. Also ask if the seller is, in fact, a dealer. If so, and the ad you're responding to hasn't clearly stated the fact, proceed cautiously.

Telephone the National Highway Traffic Safety Administration's Office of Consumer Services (800-424-9393) to find out if cars of the model year you are considering have ever been recalled. To see if a recall involves a car you're considering, get the car's vehicle identification number (VIN). If it's GM- or Ford-made, check at a local dealer; for other makes, contact the manufacturer. You can then ask the seller to show you documents that indicate the defect was fixed.

You can't recognize a real bargain unless you know the going prices for specific models. A good source of such information is the "N.A.D.A. (National Automobile Dealers Association) Official Used Car Guide." You can find it at most public libraries and banks. The guide, updated monthly, gives prices for models in average shape with average mileage (about 14,000 miles a year). A cream puff will cost more, a jalopy less.

Never buy a used car without carefully checking its performance and health on the lot, on the road, and in a diagnostic center or a trustworthy mechanic's shop.

AUTOMOBILE BATTERIES

When your car won't start, the battery usually gets the blame. But it's often something else that causes the problem. A run-down battery may have been let down by a defect in the charging system.

Have the battery checked at a repair shop with a hydrometer or a voltmeter, and be sure the battery connections are secure. If no problems show up, have a mechanic look at the starter motor, the solenoid switch, the ignition switch, and the wiring.

Battery maintenance. To avoid battery problems:

• Keep the battery firmly secured. Vibration and shock are not good for a battery's health. But don't overtighten the hold-down assembly or you may crack the battery's case.

• Be careful with tools and other metal objects. Don't, for instance, lay a wrench across both battery terminals or between the positive terminal and a metal surface. The battery could short-circuit and spray destructive acid in all directions.

• Keep lighted cigarettes and flame away from a battery. Even sparks can ignite the gas that vents from a battery's case and cause an explosion.

• Be sure any electrical connections to the battery are clean and tight. Wash off corrosive deposits, using a tablespoon of baking soda dissolved in a cup of water. (Don't let any of the solution get into battery cells.)

• Use booster cables correctly. Reversing the connections can damage the battery and the car's electrical system; it may even cause an explosion. The terminals on most batteries are marked—"+" on the positive, " — " on the negative. Also, the positive terminal is slightly thicker than the negative one.

● Check the alternator belt regularly (a mechanic can show you which one it is). Replace the belt if it's cracked or frayed—a loose belt can keep the charging system from doing its job. To find out if you need a new belt, press your thumb against it, moderately hard, at a point halfway between the two pulleys. The belt should deflect only a half-inch or so.

● If your battery isn't of the sealed, "maintenance-free" type, pull off the water caps on top from time to time. Pour in a little tap water if the battery's water isn't at the proper level.

AUTOMOBILE LEASING

Leasing a car usually isn't as good a deal as ownership. True, monthly lease payments may be lower than installment-buying payments. But if you buy, you own a car worth considerable money when it's paid up. If you lease, you own nothing after the same period.

People who lease a car usually don't avoid the normal responsibilities of ownership, either. They must still pay for insurance and maintenance. Under some contracts, they will also be charged for any unusual damage the car suffers while in their possession.

MOTOR OIL

Oil is an engine's lifeblood—it seals, cools, cleanses, lubricates, and helps fight corrosion. But you must use the proper product for your car and climate. The label on the container tells what you need to know.

The Society of Automotive Engineers (SAE) sets many motor-oil standards. The letters and numbers following the "SAE" on an oil container define the oil's viscosity gràde. For example, oil labeled *SAE 10W-30* is a multigrade oil. The first number refers to flow properties (the lower the number, the thinner the oil). The second number tells the high-temperature flow properties. The *W* denotes an oil recommended for winter use.

Oil thins out, sometimes undesirably, as it heats

up. So multigrade oils contain additives called viscosity-index improvers. Those additives make a multigrade oil behave like a relatively thick SAE 30 oil when warm.

However, some viscosity additives can cause damaging deposits. A 10W-40 oil contains more viscosity additives than a 10W-30 oil. It's best to stay away from multigrade oils with a wide spread in numbers, such as 10W-50. Use the narrowest spread that's suitable for the climate in your area.

If the container says "Energy Conserving," the oil probably has friction-modifier additives that can help improve fuel economy by a fraction of a mile per gallon.

Most oil containers also carry an API (American Petroleum Institute) symbol that refers to performance or service level. Take *API Service SF/CC*, for example. The *S* means the oil is suitable for gasoline engines. The next letter, on a scale from A to G, indicates the oil's performance level. Some oils also carry a designation such as *API Service CC* or *DD*. The *C* means the oil is suitable for diesel engines; the performance scale runs from A to D. (CD is designed for more severe service than CC.)

For gasoline engines, the SF performance level is the latest and contains a complete package of additives. In cars made before the SF level was introduced, the owner's manual may recommend an earlier level, such as SE or SD. SF oils may be used—and, in fact, are preferable—in such cars.

To increase an engine's life expectancy, change its oil frequently—every three months or 3,000 miles is a good rule of thumb. If you have a choice, use a 10W-30 oil. It can give slightly better fuel economy than 10W-40 oil and, while under stress, can provide a thicker film between moving parts than most 5W-30 oils. Also, the thicker film provided by a 10W-30 oil will benefit an older engine.

Buy motor oil for the lowest price available. Discount stores sell the same oil as service stations.

AUTOMOBILE POLISH

Paint, not polish, is what protects a car's finish. So be careful not to polish away the car's paint when restoring a smooth finish. If your buffing cloth picks up much color from the finish you're rubbing, the polish contains an abrasive that's grinding away the paint. (This test won't work on a very new car, which may have a clear top coat over the paint.)

For a very weathered finish, however, even an abrasive polish may not be adequate. You can usually find special abrasive polishing or rubbing compounds next to auto polishes on store shelves. But don't rub too hard or too long with them, or you may rub right through the paint.

Other tips:

• Whichever polish you use, wash the car thoroughly first. Most road dirt is a good deal harder than a car's finish. If you polish a dirty car, you'll grind dirt into the paint, causing small but unsightly scratches.

• A polish that has dried too long on the surface can be hard to buff. On a dry, hot day, polish can dry very quickly, so tackle only small sections at a time.

• To see whether a polish is holding up, observe what happens to water on the car's surface. The beads of water that form on a well-sealed surface are rounded and have a very small contact area. As the polish wears away, the beads spread and flatten. When the polish is completely gone, water doesn't bead at all; it lies in a sheet on the surface.

• Although you may not need to polish a new car, wash it often. Bird and tree droppings, salt, tar, and even plain dirt can eventually mar the finish. Frequent washing is especially important in the summer, when high temperatures increase the damaging effects of contaminants.

AUTOMOBILE SERVICE CONTRACTS

Plain logic suggests that automobile service contracts are apt to be poor buys. Contract-sellers make money only if buyers pay more for the warranty than they collect in claims. Of course, that's true of almost any insurance arrangement. But in the case of health insurance or homeowners insurance, you should accept the unfavorable odds because a lengthy hospitalization or the effects of a tornado can be financially devastating. That's not the case if your car's transmission breaks down.

If you worry about an unexpected major repair bill, one alternative to a service contract is to build a separate fund to pay for major repairs—"self-insuring," as some people call it. That way you keep your money if nothing goes wrong.

If you do opt for a service contract, make sure you can cancel it, just in case you have second thoughts. Most contracts allow you to cancel during the first 30, 60, or 90 days and get most of your money back. After that, you can still cancel, but you'll be charged for the time the contract was in effect and for any claim already made. You may also be charged an administrative fee of approximately $25.

In any case, don't let yourself be pressured into buying a service contract, especially when you purchase a new car. During that first year you get very little for your money, considering most new-car warranty provisions. Also, regardless of where you shop for a service contract, insist on getting the actual contract, not just a summary, and read it carefully before signing.

AUTOMOBILE WARRANTIES

Some automakers provide "secret" warranties, informal extensions of the regular car warranty, usually to cover components that have proved particularly troublesome. These extensions are often hard to discover, since the carmakers usually pass the word to their field representatives or dealers while leaving car owners in the dark.

If your car is suffering from a problem that might be covered by a secret warranty, send a self-addressed envelope with 39 cents postage to the Center for Auto Safety, 2001 S Street, N.W., Suite 410, Washington, DC 20009. The Center assembles information about secret warranties by gathering automakers' dealer bulletins and by cataloging reports from car owners. Describe your car and the problem you are experiencing, and the Center will send you specific information.

If you can't resolve the problem with the dealer's service manager, contact the nearest factory regional office listed in the car owner's manual. Follow the procedure in the manual. Often an arbitration panel may take your case. As a last resort, consider suing the dealer in small-claims court.

CAR RENTALS

There are three rental-rate schedules that cover virtually all car rentals in the U.S.—ordinary daily rates, reduced weekend rates, and weekly rates. Whichever rate you choose, you'll probably be charged by time, not mileage. "Unlimited mileage" has become a common selling point for most car-rental agencies. A few regional and local rental companies still offer time-plus-mileage rates or daily rates with a specified maximum number of "free" miles.

If you want to rent your car in one city and drop it off in another, the cost may increase substantially. Some smaller companies won't allow a one-way rental. Many of the larger ones will do one-way rentals only for certain locations—and tack on a hefty surcharge.

Collision damage waiver. The renter will usually try to pressure you to buy a "collision damage waiver" (CDW). The CDW acts like a miniature insurance policy, providing day-to-day coverage. Technically, however, the CDW is not insurance, and it is not regulated as such. (Insurance pays you money after a mishap. The CDW keeps someone from demanding money from you.)

A CDW generally costs several dollars a day, sometimes equaling or exceeding the cost of the car rental. One car-rental executive has said candidly that the CDW system is really a technique for raising the cost of the rental above the advertised rental rates.

Your personal automobile-insurance policy may also cover rental-car damage. The deductible may be the same as if you were driving your own car. In that case, you may be able to save money by turning down the CDW. Unfortunately, some insurance policies cover rental-car damage only up to $500 or $1,000. Check your policy or ask your insurance agent before you rent a car—and be sure when you travel to take along the agent's name and telephone number, the name of your insurance company, and your policy number. It's also a good idea to ask your credit-card companies if your annual card fee includes CDW coverage.

CDW coverage is incomplete as well as overpriced. The rental contract typically voids any CDW benefit if the car is driven on unpaved roads, is used to tow a boat or trailer, or is driven by an unauthorized person.

Which rental company? Most companies differ little, so shop for the least expensive rental you can find. Comparison shopping is easy: There are toll-free national reservation lines. Your travel agent can also display a full range of options on a computer screen.

Second-tier companies aren't necessarily cheaper than the major companies. Rates vary from month to month and from place to place, and discounts are widely available. You may well qualify for a significant discount through an auto club, professional society, or other association membership.

TIRE PRESSURE GAUGES

Improperly inflated tires can cause poor handling, blowouts, even high-speed accidents. Significantly underinflated tires will wear unevenly and too fast. They'll also flex too much, causing overheating and possibly early failure. Overinflated tires also wear unevenly, give a harsher ride, and cause handling problems or blowouts.

Buy yourself a good pencil-shaped gauge, one for each car you own. Keep it in the glove compartment and use it once a month or so. It will safeguard the life of your tires and help insure safe driving.

You can't rely on a gas station's air hose—the air dispenser may not be accurate. What's more, if you've driven any distance to the station, your tires will have warmed and increased their pressure by up to four to six pounds per square inch.

The recommended pressure for your car's tires (the *maximum* pressure is embossed directly on the tire sidewall) is usually for cold readings. A tire gauge lets you read the pressure right in your own driveway. If tires are underinflated, you can then drive to the filling station and inflate each tire by the requisite number of pounds, using the tire gauge as the measuring instrument.

While you are checking, don't neglect the spare. Air slowly seeps through the pores of any tire: A spare sitting in the trunk can become so underinflated as to be useless.

★ 3 ★

Protecting Your Pocketbook

CHECKING ACCOUNTS

Banks once generally provided the same checking and savings service to all customers, small or large. No more. But if you shop around, you can still find checking-account bargains.

To shop for a better-than-average checking account, look over your checkbook for several months last year—say, January, May, August, and November. Figure out how many checks you usually write and your typical balance. Then you can realistically shop for an account in a way that will minimize bank fees.

Smaller banks and savings institutions offer some of the best deals. Use the checklist below to make comparisons.

1. Name of bank: _____
2. Covered by Federal Deposit Insurance?
   ___ Yes
   ___ No
3. Type of checking account:
   ___ Regular
   ___ NOW
   ___ Super-NOW
4. Interest rate paid on account balance:
   ___ No interest
   ___ $5\frac{1}{4}$ percent
   ___ Other fixed percentage: ___ percent
   ___ Split rate: ___ percent on first $___ in account, ___ percent on amount above that.

5. Do I have to pay fees on this account?
   ___ No
   ___ Yes
   ___ Depends on balance kept in account
6. If fees depend on balance, how is balance calculated for this purpose?
   (Average daily balance is best.)
   ___ Minimum balance
   ___ Average daily balance
   ___ Other: _____
7. When fees apply, what are they?
   ___ Monthly maintenance charge: $___ per month
   ___ Fee for each check written: $___ per check
   ___ Other fees: _____
8. If interest is paid, on what balance is the interest calculated?
   ___ Interest paid daily on that day's balance
   ___ Average daily balance
   ___ Other: _____
9. What is the charge (if any) for:
   Bouncing a check (insufficient funds):
   $_____
   A certified check: $_____
   Making a deposit: $_____
   Using an automated teller machine:
   $_____
   Printing 200 checks with name and address:
   $_____
10. Convenience factors:
   How close is nearest branch to my home?
   _____

   How close is nearest branch to my office?
   _____

   Number of branches: _____
   Number of automated-teller machines:
   _____

   Bank hours: _____

FINANCIAL PLANNING

Financial planners now offer middle-income folks strategies for cutting taxes, choosing investments, and the like. Planners may work out of a home office, or they may be affiliated with well-known companies and work out of a Wall Street skyscraper. Some are lawyers or accountants who write financial plans as a sideline.

You can also buy financial plans from insurance companies or brokerage firms. In some cases, you sit down with a planner and chat about your financial needs. In others, you fill out a questionnaire and get your plan in the mail.

Planning inevitably leads to the purchase of financial products—stocks, bonds, certificates of deposit, insurance policies, etc. Many planners therefore often turn out to have hidden agendas—to sell mutual funds, for example, or life insurance, or tax-preparation services.

Here are some hallmarks of a well-drawn plan:

- It is understandably written.
- The recommendations are clear.
- It contains a cash-flow analysis (a kind of budget) that shows your income from all sources, minus all your expenses.
- There is a net-worth statement (a summary of your assets and liabilities).
- It examines your current debts to see if they should be consolidated, paid off from other available funds, or refinanced.
- It examines your current insurance and recommends ways to bolster your coverage (if necessary) and to save on premiums (if possible).
- It examines your current investment portfolio and makes recommendations for restructuring your investments, if appropriate.
- It includes a tax analysis and tax-saving suggestions.
- It touches on retirement planning and estate planning.
- It includes a statement of your goals, objectives, and tolerance for investment risk.

Instead of planning and running, a planner should help you put recommendations into effect, perhaps by coordinating the plan with others such as a lawyer, who might draw up a will for you. There should be a periodic review of the plan to see if changing circumstances have made the plan, or parts of it, obsolete.

HOUSEHOLD RECORD-KEEPING

Your current financial papers should all be in one place, easy to get to and easy to use. When records are no longer current, demote them to a dead-storage file in a closet or the attic. You also need a safe place to keep important papers—a safety-deposit box or, at the least, a fireproof strongbox. A record of how you've arranged your documents can also be useful. See the list on pages 30–31 for tips on how to organize important records.

You can throw away many records eventually. The rules of the Internal Revenue Service are often the determining factor. The previous three years are fair game for its routine audits, six years if income was significantly underreported; forever if fraud is involved.

Keep indefinitely any record related to capital improvements on your home. Their cost reduces the taxable capital gain due when you sell your house and don't reinvest the profits in another house—a liability you may face decades from now.

LIFE INSURANCE

There are huge differences among insurance policies. Here's how to sort out what you need:

Estimating insurance needs. Don't depend on an agent; figure your insurance needs yourself with the worksheet on page 29.

Affordable insurance. There are three basic types of life insurance. *Term* insurance usually provides the greatest coverage for the lowest cost. *Whole life* premiums are generally the most expensive. *Universal life* policies often cost less than whole life ones but more than term. Term premiums do rise as you get older, but they usually don't reach the level of whole life premiums for many years; by that time, you may need little or no coverage. Avoid combination plans of term with whole life or universal insurance. They're a way for the company to hook you to the "permanent" coverage it really wants to sell.

Insurance as savings. A life-insurance policy is not a very liquid investment. High start-up costs virtually lock you into a universal life or whole life policy for several years. Still, universal life policies appear to have better rates of return in the early years than whole life policies. Universal life is also more flexible, but you must pay attention to every communiqué from the insurance company to be sure the policy isn't in danger of lapsing.

WORKSHEET: HOW MUCH LIFE INSURANCE DO YOU NEED?

What You Need
Immediate expenses

Federal estate taxes		$ _____
State inheritance taxes		_____
Probate costs		_____
Funeral costs		_____
Uninsured medical costs		_____
Total final expenses	$ _____	
Future expenses		
Family expense fund		_____
Emergency fund		_____
Child-care expenses		_____
Education fund		_____
Repayment of debts		_____
Total future expenses	$ _____	
Total needs	$ _____	

What You Have Now

Cash and savings	_____
Equity in real estate	_____
Securities	_____
IRA and Keogh plans	_____
Employer savings plans, e.g. 401(k)	_____
Lump-sum employer pension benefits	_____
Current life insurance	_____
Other assets	_____
Total Assets	$ _____

Extra Insurance Needed
Total needs minus total assets

Total needs	$ _____
Total assets	_____
Additional insurance needed	_____

Dividend-paying insurance. A "participating" policy pays dividends, a partial return of your premiums. Premiums for a participating policy are generally higher than for a nonparticipating one. Dividends on term insurance are apt to be small, so it hardly matters whether the policy is participating or not. And universal life policies are priced to pay

Document	Where to Keep	How Long
Canceled checks and bank statements; records of itemized deductions (interest, medical, etc.) and depreciated equipment	Current file Dead storage	One year Five years
Credit-card numbers	Current file	Keep current
Contracts	Safe-deposit box and lawyer	Until expiration
Household inventory	Safe-deposit box and current file	Keep up-to-date
Insurance policies	Current file (policy number in safe-deposit box)	Indefinitely for life insurance; until expiration for others
Loans and promissory notes	Current file	Until paid off
Medical records	Current file	Keep up-to-date
Mortgage records and home-improvement receipts	Safe-deposit box and current file	As long as you own home or roll over profits into new home

Net-worth statements	Current file	Indefinitely
Personal records—birth certificates, marriage and divorce papers, military-service papers	Safe-deposit box	Indefinitely
Real-estate deeds	Safe-deposit box	Until property is sold
Receipts for major purchases	Current file	As long as you own the item
Stock or bond certificates	Safe-deposit box or broker	Until sold
Tax returns	Current file / Dead storage	Three years / Three years or more
Vehicle titles	Safe-deposit box	Until vehicle is sold or junked
Warranties	Current file	Until expiration
Will	Safe-deposit box and lawyer	Indefinitely

no dividends. Dividends are important mainly with whole life. A participating whole life policy is likely to be a better buy than a nonparticipating one.

Which company? In general, buy from a company rated A+ or A by Best's Insurance Reports, available in many libraries.

Comparison shopping. Ask three or four agents to present one or more policies of the type you want. Compare interest-adjusted net cost indexes (if it's a term or a whole life policy you want). The lower the index, the less costly the policy.

Bigger doesn't necessarily mean better. Some of the best buys are from small or medium-size companies.

The agent. You may not mind paying a little more for a policy to keep the services of an agent who's attentive to your needs, explains policy details clearly, and puts your family's interests ahead of his or her commission income. Service may be especially important with a universal life policy—a good agent will contact you periodically to check if the policy still meets your needs or if you should consider adjustments in coverage.

MAIL-ORDER SHOPPING AND FRAUD

Most mail-order companies will act quickly to rectify problems, but some may not. If you run into trouble, write a letter to the company explaining what went wrong with your order. If you telephone to complain, write a follow-up letter. If you don't hear in 30 days, write to other agencies:

• *Direct Marketing Association,* 6 E. 43rd St., New York, NY 10017. The DMA sponsors a Mail Order Action Line that will intervene on your behalf and refer you to other agencies.

• *Better Business Bureau,* Council of Better Business Bureaus Inc., 1515 Wilson Blvd., Arlington, VA 22209, 703-276-0100. The BBB can help you check a company's reputation before you order, and it accepts complaints thereafter. You must contact the BBB office nearest the company's headquarters, not the office in your area. To get a directory of BBB offices, contact the council at the address above.

• *Federal Trade Commission,* Pennsylvania Ave. & 6th St., N.W., Washington, DC 20580, 202-326-2180. The FTC does not act on individual complaints, but it does use them to build cases against companies.

● State and local consumer-protection agencies may also be able to help resolve your problem.

Mail-order fraud. To avoid becoming a fraud victim:

● Read advertisements carefully, especially the fine print. Don't rely on pictures and headlines.

● Always pay by check, money order, or credit card so you have a receipt of payment.

● Don't order from an unfamiliar company if an advertisement lists only a post-office box; the company may not want to disclose its exact location.

● Don't order from companies that *require* the use of toll-free "800" numbers and charge cards. They may be trying to avoid use of the mails to get around federal postal laws.

● Beware of high-pressure tactics—"can't miss" deals, "last time" offers, "once in a lifetime" opportunities, and "limited supply" sales.

● Keep all advertisements, envelopes, and correspondence with a company in case you have complaints about your order. (Some firms require that you send in the original ad with your order. In that case, copy the ad before sending it in.) If you order by phone, make a record of the order—price, time, and date of your conversation, and the name of the person you talked with.

MORTGAGE PAYMENTS

Whether you already have a mortgage or are in the market for a new one, you can probably save tens of thousands of dollars by "investing" in your mortgage. Several new types of mortgage have an accelerated payment schedule. By cutting the loan's term to reduce interest payments, you may net more money than by earning interest on more liquid investments.

Rather than spending or investing elsewhere, consider plowing cash back into savings in your house. With a little discipline, you can probably squeeze out slightly more money each month to help prepay the existing mortgage. Even considering the lost tax deduction and the lost income the extra payments could have earned in other investments, you are still apt to come out ahead.

To prepay, you merely notify a lender to apply the extra amount directly to repayment of principal, not for interest. You may want to write a separate check to ensure that the lender services your loan properly. Keep track of how much extra principal you've paid, and compare your figures with the year-end statement issued by your mortgage holder.

MOVING

If you move, one thing you can expect is a big bill. Not very long ago, the average household move (transporting some 6,000 pounds about 1,100 miles) cost more than $2,500.

Most moving vans haul the belongings of more than one customer. To determine the weight of your things, the mover weighs the truck, with whatever load is already on it, on a certified scale, then loads your things and weighs the truck again. What you pay depends on the difference between the initial weight (the "tare") and the weight after loading (the "gross").

You can often save by getting at least three estimates. There are three types of estimate—binding, nonbinding, and a hybrid of the two. With a binding estimate, the estimated cost is final; the mover won't even weigh your things on moving day. A binding estimate is generally the best kind, even though it may be slightly higher than a nonbinding one. A nonbinding estimate is desirable only if, at the time of the estimate, you're still unsure about what you'll be moving.

Many movers also offer an estimate that binds them but not you. Under that arrangement, the mover issues a binding estimate but weighs your things on moving day anyway. If the actual weight of your shipment is more than estimated, you pay only the estimated rate. If the weight is less, you pay only for the actual weight.

The mover you choose will draw up an "order for service." That isn't a contract: If you delay your move or decide not to use the company, you can cancel without a penalty. You'll sign the actual contract, the "bill of lading," on packing day—or moving day, if you're doing the packing yourself.

Don't sign an order for service or a bill of lading

unless it mentions specific dates for pickup and delivery. If a mover fails to pick up or deliver on time, you may be able to collect for out-of-pocket expenses during the delay by filing an inconvenience or delay claim with your mover.

Damage. Before moving, check whether your homeowners insurance policy covers your possessions for damage or loss during the move. If not, you can usually get coverage from your insurance company or the mover. Should anything be lost or damaged, get a claim form from your agent or from the mover's home office. The sooner you file, the sooner you have a chance to collect. But in any case, your claim must be filed within nine months.

If you can't resolve a dispute through the regular claims process, you can take the moving company to court. Or you can request arbitration, by writing the American Movers Conference, Dispute Settlement Program, 400 Army-Navy Drive, Arlington, VA 22202. Your letter must be sent within 60 days after the final offer or denial on your claim has been made in writing by the mover. The decision is supposed to be made within 60 days of receipt of all necessary forms.

MUTUAL FUNDS

A welter of mutual funds compete for your investment dollars. How can you identify good performers?

The Standard and Poor's index of 500 stocks is a useful yardstick. A fund worthy of your money should outperform the S & P in most years. A fund salesperson should be able to show you, in writing, how a particular fund has done compared with the S & P 500. You might also want to send for recent prospectuses and compare funds on your own.

Here are six types of stock mutual funds:

• *Balanced funds* invest in a fairly even mixture of stocks and bonds.
• *Income funds* invest in a flexible mixture of bonds and stocks that pay high dividends.
• *Long-term growth funds* (also called ''growth funds'') invest in stocks of companies with rising earnings. The primary objective of a growth fund is capital gains (appreciation in the price of the stocks, as opposed to dividends).

• *Growth-and-income funds* aim for a balance between dividends and capital gains.

• *Maximum-capital-gains funds* (also called "aggressive growth funds") try for the highest possible capital gains. They differ from growth funds by investing in the shares of smaller companies, or by using borrowed money in an attempt to magnify investment results, or both.

• *Specialized funds* invest in a narrowly defined sector, such as gold and gold mining.

The following two types of funds are not stock funds:

• *Money market funds* invest in large bank certificates of deposit and short-term IOU's issued by corporations and government agencies. The risk is negligible. While solid yields are virtually assured, spectacular gains, like those sometimes achieved with stock funds, are essentially precluded.

• *Bond funds* involve more risk than money market funds, because bonds can rise and fall in value. In general, the potential gains or losses from a bond fund are smaller than those with a stock fund.

PERSONAL SECURITY

A few simple steps can help protect you from street crime. The National Crime Prevention Council recommends that men carry a wallet in their front pants pocket to thwart pickpockets, rather than in their back pocket or front jacket pocket. Or consider a money belt—few muggers think of asking victims to remove their belts, except in places like Las Vegas where the belts are common.

You might choose a wallet with a fabric exterior, which is tougher to remove from a pocket than a slick leather one. Finally, keep your cash and credit cards separate.

The NCPC advises women to carry a wallet with important identification and credit cards in a pocket separate from their handbag, and to use a handbag with a long strap worn across the body.

SAVINGS ACCOUNTS

How do you shop for a savings account? Here are helpful things to know:

• *Annual percentage rate.* The APR is the basic yearly interest rate that the account pays.

• *Compounding.* The more frequent the compounding period, the better off you are. However, continuous compounding yields only a tiny bit more than daily compoundings.

• *Yield.* The annual percentage yield takes into consideration both the APR and the frequency of compounding. It tells you by what percentage a deposit will grow if you leave it in the account for a full year.

• *Balance method.* How does a financial institution determine the amount on which interest is paid? The fairest method is called day-of-deposit to day-of-withdrawal (sometimes known as day-in to day-out, or DIDO), which pays interest each day on the actual balance in your account. Another common method is day-of-deposit to end-of-interest-period; withdrawals before the end of the interest period (usually the end of the month) don't earn interest for any of that period. Least fair is the low-balance method. This system pays you interest only on the lowest balance in your account during the interest period, and ignores the rest.

• *Fees, charges, and penalties.* If your balance falls below a certain minimum, is there a service charge or do you cease to earn interest? Is there a charge for withdrawals after a certain number is reached? Is there a charge for so-called inactive accounts? What other special charges are there?

• *Delaying interest on deposits.* Does the financial institution start paying interest the day checks are deposited, or does it wait for the check to clear?

• *Deposit insurance.* Be sure to check whether you would be covered by federal deposit insurance. Unless you're in a position to judge the adequacy of a state deposit-insurance fund, stick with a federally insured institution.

TELEPHONE FRAUD

Each year, high-pressure telephone salespeople cheat consumers in a big way. Con artists promote precious metals, phony investments, rare coins, stamps, currency contracts, oil and gas leases, artwork—anything a trusting investor is willing to buy.

If you think you have been victimized or are considering an investment with an unfamiliar firm, contact these authorities:

• *Commodities Futures Trading Commission.* To find out if the CFTC has filed any litigation against a company, call 202-254-8630. To file a complaint against a futures company or to find out if there have been other consumer complaints, call the CFTC at 202-254-3060.

• *Federal Trade Commission.* To find out if the FTC has taken action against a company or to file a complaint, call 202-326-2222.

• *National Association of Securities Dealers.* For additional information on a securities firm, call the NASD at 301-738-6500.

• *National Futures Association.* All futures companies trading on the futures exchange must be registered. To find out if a commodities company is registered, call the NFA at 800-621-3570. Just because a company is registered doesn't mean it's legitimate.

• *Securities and Exchange Commission.* To find out if the SEC has taken action against a particular company, call 202-272-7440.

• *State and local authorities.* Before investing, consider contacting the Better Business Bureau in your state and the state where the offer was made.

★ 4 ★

Making the Most of Your Leisure

AIRLINE OVERBOOKING

Almost all airlines overbook—they sell more tickets for a given flight than they have seats. The federal government allows the practice because up to 20 percent of all passengers who reserve seats don't show up. But you have certain rights if you're denied a seat on a flight you've paid for.

If a flight is overbooked, federal regulations require that the airline ask for volunteers who are willing to take a later flight. The airline will offer some sort of compensation, usually a coupon good for a free domestic flight. Don't volunteer unless you're given a confirmed seat on an acceptable substitute flight. If you're merely put on standby or on a waiting list, you might not get on that plane either.

If there aren't enough volunteers, the airline will systematically deny boarding to certain passengers, usually on a first-come, first-served basis. If you are involuntarily bumped, you may be entitled to compensation. The amount depends on how late you arrive at your original destination.

If you have been bumped from a flight because of overbooking and believe you have been treated unfairly, call the U.S. Department of Transportation, Office of Community and Consumer Affairs, at 202-366-2220, or write to 400 7th St., S.W., Washington, DC 20590.

BATTERIES—DRY CELL

Do the many batteries used in various gadgets confuse you? Here's a rundown on the types you're most likely to come across:

• *Zinc carbon.* This is an inexpensive, general-purpose battery that discharges quickly, deteriorates rapidly at high temperature—and doesn't work well in the cold. Many of these have an inner zinc casing that is eaten away as the battery is used and leaks a corrosive paste.

• *Zinc chloride.* These batteries are usually labeled "heavy duty." They last longer than zinc-carbon batteries and operate over a wider temperature range.

• *Alkaline.* Technically called *alkaline manganese batteries,* these batteries use alkaline rather than acidic chemicals. They cost three to five times as much as zinc-carbon or zinc-chloride batteries, but they last up to 10 times as long. Alkaline batteries are good for motorized toys, cassette players, and electronic flash units. They have a long shelf life and are tolerant of temperature extremes.

• *Nickel cadmium.* The chemical reaction that produces electricity in these batteries can be reversed with a battery charger. Since these batteries are expensive, and you have to buy a charger, they are impractical for devices that you use only occasionally. The best candidates for their use are devices that require a lot of power and that get regular use, such as walkabout tape players.

• *Button batteries.* These tiny batteries work well in low-power devices such as hearing aids, watches, cameras, and calculators with a liquid crystal display.

• *Lithium.* Batteries that use this metal are expensive. However, button batteries made with lithium pack a lot of power in a small package and are claimed to have a shelf life as long as 10 years.

Cautions in use. Dry-cell batteries demand precautions:

• Metal can short-circuit a battery, creating enough heat to cause a burn. Don't let batteries touch anything metallic, including keys in your pocket or purse, or tools in a hardware drawer.

• Batteries can explode. Don't burn them or put them with trash to be incinerated.

• Zinc-carbon and zinc-chloride batteries keep longer if refrigerated.

• Keep batteries—especially small button batteries—away from children.

• Don't recharge batteries that weren't made for that purpose.

• Don't mix batteries of different types: The strong batteries will put stress on the weak ones, and may cause them to leak.

• A set of batteries will produce only as much power as the weakest battery allows, so change all batteries in a device at the same time.

CAMCORDERS

In one convenient package the camcorder gives you everything you need to shoot a scene and play it back on your TV set. For most people, though, choosing a camcorder involves a trip into unknown territory. You'll do well to buy a unit with the following attributes:

• A zoom lens that provides at least a 6:1 zoom ratio.

• An electronic viewfinder designed to be used with either eye.

• Controls that automatically adjust the white balance of the picture.

• Controls that let you adjust the focus and lens opening automatically. The automatic controls on many camcorders aren't ideal for every situation.

A camcorder should also be easy to hold, with the controls conveniently placed. Larger models may seem bulky and cumbersome at first, but they rest on a shoulder in use, which makes it easier to hold the camera steady. Small, hand-held camcorders are neither easier nor harder to use than the larger models. The small ones are easier to carry, but they may yield shakier pictures. For long takes, a tripod is useful for any camcorder.

CAMERAS

Before you buy a camera, ask yourself this question: Do you need advanced equipment or just something for snapshots?

A 35 millimeter (mm) single-lens reflex (SLR)

camera lets the photographer see what the camera "sees" (through whichever lens is being used) and thus compose a shot precisely. However, an SLR may be more camera than you really need or want. If you take pictures only on vacations and special occasions, you'll probably be happier with a simpler, less costly camera. Similarly, if you don't necessarily want to explore the variety of interchangeable lenses available for SLRs, there's little point to owning one. Nevertheless, if you're a shutterbug who wants the latest and the best, you will certainly want to consider an *autofocus* model.

The most automatic SLRs not only focus themselves with remarkable speed and precision, they also help with loading and winding film and with setting the shutter speed and aperture. These features let beginners get professional-level results in most situations. Most of the automated cameras can still be used manually, so that advanced photographers can retain creative control.

However, if you already know how to use an SLR or are willing to learn, you can find good value in a manual-focus SLR.

For beginners. Up until fairly recently, if you wanted a simple point-and-shoot camera, you had to buy a disc or 110-size product. Those cameras produce small negatives that don't enlarge well beyond snapshot size.

The newer, automated, compact 35mm camera is just about as small and as easy to use as any disc or 110 camera, but it delivers the quality inherent in the larger frame of 35mm film.

Most compact cameras make picture-taking easy with features like these:

• Automatic load: You drop in the film cartridge, pull some film out, and a motor threads and winds the film through. The same motor advances the film after each shot and rewinds when the roll is finished.

• Automatic exposure control: This helps prevent pictures from coming out too light or dark. A compact usually "reads" the film's sensitivity from the metallic coding on the film cartridge and adjusts the camera accordingly.

• Built-in flash: Fires when it is needed.

• Automatic focus.

Unlike a single-lens reflex, a compact 35mm camera doesn't let you see precisely what you are shooting. You have to learn to leave a little more space at crucial points in the image to avoid cutting off tops of heads and the like.

Other limitations of these cameras concern the advanced photographer more than the snapshooter. The exposure settings, for instance, are decided by the camera, not you—a trade of control for convenience. On the other hand, a compact 35mm camera is smaller and lighter than a single-lens reflex. That counts for a lot when traveling.

CARRY-ON LUGGAGE

The bag you carry onto an airplane is the one you don't have to wait for later in the baggage claim area. A soft or semisoft bag (also see Soft-sided luggage, page 50) has an advantage in airplanes with little underseat room because it can be forced into place. (If you stuff the bag too full to go under the seat, you can always use an overhead bin.)

Here's what to look for in soft luggage:

Handles. In bags that have two strap handles, you should be able to join the handles together with a wraparound flap secured by snaps or Velcro. The flap's size is important: A flap narrower than your palm may dig into your hand. A flap that doesn't easily wrap around the handles quickly becomes a bother to use. Strap handles that lack a flap fall to the sides of the bag when you put it down. Every time you pick up the bag, you have to gather up the straps—a nuisance.

Rigid-frame bags and some semisoft bags have a conventional suitcase handle. The most comfortable handles of that type have padding at the bottom.

Shoulder straps. When your hands are busy with tickets, reading material, or other paraphernalia, a shoulder strap is a boon. The strap should have a pad with a textured surface that provides friction so the strap doesn't slip from your shoulder. A shoulder strap should be removable.

Floor. A floor helps to distribute the weight of a bag's contents. A soft floor, without any stiffening, is not very effective. A floor attached inside the bag on only one side can be tipped up to let the bag collapse for storage.

Compartments. A handy design features a wide center compartment flanked by narrower ones. Pockets that don't run the full width of a bag are for stowing miscellaneous items; a plastic-lined pocket is handy for carrying a damp swimsuit. Zippers or snap-tabs on pockets help keep things in place. Exterior pockets should have a zipper or a secure latch for stowing important items you need quick access to, such as airline tickets or medications.

Straps and hangers. Tie-down straps keep clothes folded and in place. They should be long enough to go around clothing and be easy to drape out of the way while you pack.

Zippers. Plastic zippers operate much more smoothly than metal. Double-pull zippers should go around three sides of a bag, to let you open just one side of the bag to fish something out or unzip the bag all the way for convenient packing and unpacking.

Style and appearance. A light-colored bag will show dirt, and a bag of a dark color will develop a whitish haze after abrasion. Medium-intensity colors are probably best. Tweeds also hide dirt well.

COOLER CHESTS

For a once- or twice-a-summer outing, a cheap chest can do very well. Consider a foamed-plastic cooler chest—lightweight and inexpensive, though fragile. But if you are a part of a family of picnickers, it's probably better to invest in something more substantial. You may then want a "clad" cooler with a plastic or metal shell around its insulation—durable but often quite heavy.

Any chest can be made more effective with a little planning. Here are some tips:

• A block of ice melts more slowly than ice cubes. You can make your own blocks by prefreezing milk cartons of water. Or you can buy sealed, reusable containers of liquid that can be frozen for use in picnic chests.

• A chest packed with cold foods and beverages will stay cool longer than one filled with room-temperature items.

- Keep the chest away from heat sources; if direct sunlight can't be avoided, drape a blanket over the chest.

- Open the cover as little as possible and close it quickly.

FILM PROCESSING

Ordinary snapshooters have three main processing choices. They can use a mail-order processor and wait a week or so. They can drop off film at a supermarket, drugstore, camera store, or kiosk for pickup in one or two days. (Either way, the film is generally processed at a big laboratory that handles thousands of rolls a day.) A third alternative is the "minilab"—a retail outlet that does the processing on the premises and commonly offers finished prints in as little as an hour. Minilabs tend to be expensive, compared with mail-order processing.

The main drawback to mail-order film processing is slow delivery. Solving problems that require reprinting can also be awkward from a distance. And there's always a small risk in sending film through the mail.

No matter where you have film processed, machines do at least most of the labor. Examine your pictures carefully when you get them back. The following tips may help you to get the prints you want:

- If a print is unsatisfactory, check the negative. If the image has good contrast, ask to have the print remade. Give the lab clear, written instructions— "the flower should be lavender, not dark purple" or "background is dark red; print so face in foreground is normal flesh tones." Ordinarily, you won't have to pay for remakes of a bad print.

- Try to keep the film cool, particularly between exposure and development. Don't let a roll sit in the camera a month while waiting to take the last shot, and don't leave your camera or film in the sun or in an enclosed, hot car. Keep unexposed film in the refrigerator. On a vacation in a hot climate, have your pictures developed promptly. Take a mailer along and send film to a lab as it's shot.

- Handle negatives as little as possible. Never touch the part with the image. When selecting negatives for reprinting or enlargement, send the whole strip; never cut the negatives apart. Fill out the envelope before inserting the negatives.

• There's no remedy for film that's ruined by the processor. The best you can expect is a new roll, with free processing.

• If your film is lost, it may turn up later, particularly if you've labeled the cartridge with your name and address.

GAS BARBECUE GRILLS

The least efficient gas grill is cheaper to run than a kettle-type charcoal grill of similar size. Of course, a gas grill costs more to buy and may impose some hidden costs as well. The model you select should come with its own fuel tanks (otherwise, tanks cost an extra $25 or so). The tank must be purged of air before its first filling, a service that may cost you a couple of dollars. An inaccurate fuel gauge on the tank may also cost you some money, since the filling charge is the same no matter how much gas is left in the tank.

Features. A window in the lid, a temperature gauge, and a timer are frills. More important are handy shelves and racks, an easy-to-change fuel tank, and split cooking grids easier to clean than one large grid.

Assembly. Even if you are mechanically adept, you might prefer to have a dealer set up your grill; some do the job at no charge. Dealers can cope better with damaged or missing parts than you can. If possible, have the gas-pressure regulator checked and adjusted. Ask the dealer to light the grill as well. The igniter should fire the burners in at least four seconds. The burners' flames should be blue with a touch of yellow at their tips; if the flames are all blue or all soft yellow, the shutter that regulates the air/fuel ratio needs adjustment.

Cleaning. A thrifty technique: Before cooking, run the grill on High for about 15 minutes. Then put on oven mitts and scrub the grids with a soft brass-bristle brush.

Safety. Follow these pointers:

• Never store a fuel tank indoors. Tanks vent gas automatically if too much pressure builds up, as it might on a hot day. Indoor gas buildups are dangerous.

• When bringing the tank home after a refill, prop it up securely. Drive with a window open.

• Keep the tank upright as you reconnect it to the grill's regulator (if it tips, a spurt of the fuel could damage the regulator). Then check the connection with a few drops of detergent solution; bubbles indicate a leak.

• Clean the grill regularly—once a year or after every 50 cookouts. Clean the burner ports, venturi tubes, and the tip of the igniter. With the gas turned off, check the igniter to be sure it sparks properly.

• Keep the grill well away from combustible surfaces, and don't position it under low eaves or overhangs.

• Never use a gas grill in a garage doorway or an enclosed porch, where escaping gas could explode.

• Use oven mitts and avoid loose-fitting clothing when lighting and using the grill.

• If you buy an extra LP (liquid petroleum) tank, buy only the kind approved by the U.S. Department of Transportation for LP gas. Never buy a used tank. Have any tank inspected professionally every five years for leaks.

HAIR CONDITIONERS

Do you long for hair that's shiny and manageable, with body and bounce? A hair conditioner can help. But some of the promises exceed the delivery.

A conditioner reduces the roughness of hair's outer surfaces, making it softer, shinier, and easier to comb. By coating each hair, the conditioner counteracts static electricity, so hair is more manageable. But "self-adjusting" conditioners, which claim to provide as much or as little conditioning as hair needs, really offer nothing special. Hair tends to take what it needs and sheds the rest.

As for providing extra body for fine hair, any conditioner coats the hair and is bound to make each strand slightly thicker. There's no consistent difference between extra-body and regular varieties of a particular brand.

A conditioner for dry or normal hair usually contains oils or fatty substances, such as mineral oil or lanolin. A formulation for oily hair usually contains "oil-free" synthetic polymers. But those special formulations don't seem to bear on how well a conditioner does its job.

Some products are claimed to provide substances that hair "craves." A product for "nourishing" hair may contain protein, wheat germ, milk, egg, or honey. But hair, once it is outside the scalp, is not a living thing. It can't be nourished. (A poor diet or poor health, however, can cause poor-looking hair.)

No conditioner can permanently repair damaged hair. It may hide split ends temporarily, by gluing them together. Protein in the conditioner may even fill in gaps in damaged hair—until you shampoo again. The only way to eliminate damaged hair is to cut it off.

Not everyone needs to condition hair after shampooing. People with short, healthy hair that has not been color-treated or permed may never need a conditioner. Some people may need a conditioner only in the winter, when there's less moisture in the air, or in summer, when exposure to salt water or chlorinated pools makes hair feel dry.

If your hair tends to be tangled, flyaway, or unmanageable after shampooing, or if you'd like it a bit softer or shinier, your hair may need more conditioning. But if it looks limp and somewhat greasy right after shampooing, you're probably conditioning too much.

INSECT REPELLENTS

Repellents work against mosquitoes, chiggers, ticks, fleas, and some biting flies. Many protect against the black fly, whose bite makes a dangerous, long-lasting wound. They don't work against ants or stinging insects like bees and wasps.

An insect repellent doesn't only keep you comfortable, it can keep you healthy. Biting pests sometimes carry serious disease: for example, mosquito-borne encephalitis and tick-borne Lyme disease and Rocky Mountain spotted fever.

The active ingredient of most products is "deet," short for N, N-diethyl-meta-toluamide. Deet is an oily and somewhat sticky liquid, available in full-concentration lotion or diluted in lotions, aerosols, pump sprays, sticks, and towelettes. You apply it to your clothing as well as directly to exposed parts of your body. When trekking into tick-infested areas, treat cuffs, socks, and shoe tops, too.

Repellents are safe on cotton, wool, and nylon. But they can damage other fabrics, particularly synthetics like spandex, rayon, and acetate. Be careful about getting any repellent on a bathing suit (often part spandex) or Hawaiian shirts (often rayon). With polyester or polyester/cotton blends, test the repellent on an inside seam; damage shows up quickly as softened or discolored material.

The compounds also mar plastics and painted or varnished surfaces. Don't touch plastic eyeglass lenses, wristwatch crystals, auto dashboards, furniture, and the like with insect repellent on your hands.

Generally, the higher the concentration of active ingredient, the longer-lasting the protection. But even the strongest formulas may need to be reapplied after an hour or two for protection against hungry bugs such as black flies.

Use repellents only when necessary, and then sparingly. Don't use a repellent on a small child, except in a heavily infested area. Even then, use only a product that contains a minimal amount of active ingredients—100 percent deet formulas are overkill.

Repellents should never be slathered onto naked limbs and torsos like sunscreens. A day or two before you plan to start using a repellent, apply a small amount to forearm or thigh. Check the spot for redness over the next 24 to 48 hours. If you find none, there aren't likely to be any skin problems with that particular formula.

Never spray aerosol or pump products directly on the face—spray into the palm of one hand and use the other hand to apply the liquid. Repellents are flammable; never spray them near lighted cigarettes, campfires, or open flames.

LIPSTICKS

No lipstick is perfect. You'll have to decide which factor is most important to you and compromise on the others. Here are a few factors to consider:

Applying and removing. A creamy or opaque lipstick is usually easier to put on than one that's waxy or sheer (lacking in opacity). A lipstick that's easy to put on is also apt to be easy to take off.

Creaminess. Creamy lipsticks moisturize lips, but they can smear and bleed. Creaminess and waxiness are usually at odds with one another.

Opacity. With an opaque lipstick, you needn't

apply a thick layer to get the color you want. Chances are, the color on your lips will also match the color in the tube. However, opaque lipsticks, especially glossy ones, can make lips look painted and less natural than sheer lipsticks.

Gloss. Glossy lipsticks give lips a shiny, wet look. But both glossy and frosted lipsticks reflect light and thus tend to accentuate flaws. If your lips are wrinkled or chapped, try a matte finish.

Blotting resistance. Creamy lipsticks normally blot off more quickly than waxy ones.

Staining. Lipsticks with a relatively high concentration of dye can stain your lips. They'll also stay on your lips longer—though the color may change as the less-permanent pigments wear off. Don't assume that the lighter colors won't stain.

Color. Choose shades to match your skin tone. Peaches, corals, "warm" pinks, and orange-reds look best on yellowish or olive skin. People whose skin has a blue undertone look good in clear reds and shades of pink.

Tips on application:

• Use a brush—especially with bright, opaque lipsticks, where precise control is critical.

• Use a lip liner to help define your lips and keep the color from feathering beyond the lip line. With pale, natural lipstick shades, match the liner closely to your lip color; with brighter shades, match the liner to the lipstick.

• To make lipstick last for several hours, blot and reapply two or three times. Finish with a light dusting of face power to set the lipstick.

SOFT-SIDED LUGGAGE

(Also see Carry-on Luggage, page 43.) Today's travelers often have to be their own porters. Light, soft-sided luggage is the kind to buy if you generally tote your own bags. There's a broad range to choose from.

Bags without any stiffness at all protect their contents the least but are quite adaptable. They can stow odd shapes, and they're fine for jeans, socks, shoes, and casual clothing. They're also very easy to store, and can be pummeled—within reason—into tight spots when packed.

"Partial-frame" bags are slightly more protective. Some have a stiff bottom panel and a suggestion of a frame—springy wires in bindings around the edge. Others have a narrow steel band around their middle that supports the handle. Empty, a bag with a partial frame can be squashed fairly flat for storage. As with a soft bag, your cargo expands the bag to its full width, so it's a bit awkward to pack and none too convenient if you have to live out of the suitcase. Its design also protects it only at limited points against rough handling.

As soft-sided luggage goes, a bag with full-width framing gives the best protection. Where a partial-width frame gives a bag a stable shape in length and height, a "full" frame gives a bag shape and protectiveness in width as well.

A full frame isn't necessarily stiff—it can range from rigid to flexible. Nor is the full-frame effect necessarily caused by a full frame. In some, the frame is a full-width band some six to eight inches wide. In others, the frame is merely about two inches wide, with plastic interior inserts at the corners to hold the bag square. That design can make a bag hard to close; you must tug and pull the lid over the inserts.

Because a full-frame bag holds its shape like a dresser drawer, it's convenient to live out of and to pack. However, the bag demands identical space whether full, partly full, or empty—a consideration if you have limited storage space.

You can do a quick in-store check of a soft-sider's rigidity by pressing firmly, then releasing, the bag's top, sides, and corners. The less it yields and the faster it rebounds, the more protection it's apt to offer. Note, however, that even the most rigid full-frame case can't be sat on or stepped on when empty.

Wheels can save work. Most wheeled bags have two swiveling wheels at front and a fixed pair at the rear.

A four-wheel case trails you like a reluctant dog, usually pulling your arm straight behind you. A two-wheeled case trundles along at your side when you lift up the front end. It takes some extra effort to keep it upended as you proceed.

Small wheels (an inch or less in diameter) on a four-wheel bag turn reluctantly on carpeting and rough surfaces. Bigger (two-inch) wheels on a two-wheeler make it easier to roll the bag along pebbly surfaces. But any wheeled bag should do well on a smooth straightaway.

Handles. Some bags have a top-mounted handle, usually some sort of single grip. Check that it provides enough clearance for your gloved hand. Other bags use side-attached handles, twin looped straps like a shopping bag's, some with a small cover that snaps over the paired straps as cushioning. If you are short, check that you can lift and carry the bag without holding your arm at a tiring angle.

Watch out for zippers secured by easy-to-unravel chain stitching. Check a bag's interior for sharp projections, and check hardware and interior fittings for proper function and secure attachment.

TELEVISION SETS

When you buy your next color TV set, give first consideration to a model that can handle stereo sound. You're likely to get a set that delivers good picture quality and very good sound in both the stereo and monophonic modes. A set with a 19- or 20-inch screen is large enough for the whole family to watch but not big enough to dominate a room.

Stereo sets are at the high end of the price spectrum. They typically include input and output jacks for such equipment as a stereo videocassette recorder and external speakers or a computer. Less expensive sets are a lot simpler, with monophonic sound, fewer accessory jacks, and, in some cases, a less-deluxe remote control. The differences between models also show up in these features:

Channel selector. The old-fashioned rotary knob tuner turns up only on the cheapest sets. Higher-priced models generally have an electronic selector that gives you "direct access": You can go directly from channel 2 to channel 9, for example.

One type of electronic tuner has to be adjusted before you can use it. The adjustment involves tedious setting of tiny buttons, dials, or switches to bring in the desired channels. Once these controls have been set, you change channels with a button or a knob. Some tuners limit the number of channels you can receive at one time—an annoyance to cable-TV users who have two dozen or more channels available. Quartz-locked tuners are best in this respect; they can receive many more of the available channels.

Remote control. On some sets, it's a necessity— some tuning, sound, and picture controls are only on the remote control, not on the TV set.

Displays. Many sets display the channel you are watching or the time of day on the TV screen at the touch of a button. But the clock feature can be a nuisance in areas with frequent power interruptions, which wipe out the set's timekeeping memory.

Auxiliary inputs and outputs. A set that can be the command center of a home-entertainment system can be more satisfactory than a basic model. Features to look for:

• An *audio output jack* lets you shut off sound from the TV set's speakers and route it directly to a hi-fi system. The jack also allows a connection to an audio tape recorder, so that you can record sound tracks or televised music programs.

• *Video and audio input jacks* provide a permanent hookup for components such as a videocassette recorder or a computer and a slightly clearer picture than you'd get with a connection through the TV set's antenna terminals.

• An *RGB (red-green-blue) input* can provide a much sharper display if you use the TV set as a computer monitor.

• *An earphone jack* that lets you hear a program without annoying others is called a muting jack. You need a nonmuting jack if you want to pipe sound directly to the ear of someone who is hard of hearing without cutting off sound to the rest of the family. Some sets have both types.

• *Cable connection.* A "cable ready" set can receive at least 23 channels reserved for nonscrambled cable programs, with no need for a cable company's converter box. You *will* need a converter box if the signal is delivered scrambled. And you'll need an "addressable decoder" to watch pay-per-view programs.

When you are tied into cable, you may find that you can't make full use of your videocassette recorder without getting some extra hardware. You may not, for example, be able to watch one program while recording another.

VIDEOCASSETTE RECORDERS

Do you want a VCR primarily for time-shifting—recording a program that you want to watch at a later time? Then you need a VCR that's easy to program and that can record all the shows you want over an extended time span. Every VCR lets you do some time-shifting; as you move up in price, you generally get greater time-shifting ability.

For playing prerecorded tapes (and limited time-shifting), the most basic VCR will do. Consider a higher-priced VCR with hi-fi sound if you want good-quality music reproduction.

A lot of people use a camcorder (a camera with a built-in video recorder) to make their own video home movies. Converting those tapes into sophisticated videos requires a fairly full-featured VCR that allows editing and sound dubbing.

Most machines use the VHS format; the Beta format is disappearing. The newer 8mm format is fine for time-shifting, but not many rental tapes are available. Because 8mm tape cassettes are so small, the format lends itself to use in portable VCRs meant for shooting home videos.

Cable TV. Most VCRs are "cable ready" in the sense that you can attach the cable directly to the machine. Truly cable-ready VCRs can receive non-scrambled cable-TV channels directly, without a cable-converter box or other hardware. The cable won't affect the VCR's time-shifting ability. You may, however, need a converter box to receive the so-called premium channels, such as HBO and Showtime.

In any VCR, these features are niceties:

● A tuner that lets you bring in any available channel easily, and that can receive all the channels in your area.

● On-screen programming, which lets you set the VCR to record automatically with a minimum of fuss and frustration.

● One-touch recording, which lets you start recording instantly.

● Auto-index, which makes it simple to find programs on a tape.

VIDEOTAPE

If you buy standard-grade videotape, you're doing the right thing. Manufacturers' grade designations don't help much in identifying the best tape. One company's "super high" grade is often no better than another company's—or even its own— "high" grade. The performance of each brand's various grades is often indistinguishable. The overall quality of brand-name videotape is quite high, regardless of grade.

Gaps, scratches, or a poorly applied coating cause the intermittent flecks and streaks called dropouts, some so short that the human eye can't see them. Additionally, all videocassette recorders have circuitry that replaces missing bits of picture lines with corresponding bits from the line above, a trick that ordinarily goes undetected by the viewer.

Sound. Up until recently, all VCRs used the "linear track" method to record sound; a narrow strip is reserved along the tape's edge for the sound track. However, the tape's low speed makes good audio quality difficult to achieve.

A few years ago, high-fidelity sound was introduced in VCRs using the tape's full width. In response, tape manufacturers introduced new tape grades with names that sound as though the tapes were engineered especially for hi-fi VCRs. In fact, almost any brand-name tape should give excellent audio results with any hi-fi VCR.

Licensed tape. The JVC and Sony companies, respective originators of the VHS and Beta tape formats, license other manufacturers to produce videotape. Those tapes carry an official VHS or Beta logo. Before buying an unfamiliar tape brand, check the packaging to see if the tape is licensed. Unlicensed tape tends to have defects—excessive dropouts, considerable noise, and the like.

Some unlicensed tapes avoid using an official logo. Others skirt the legal edge by using the logo in a sentence rather than having it stand alone. Another tipoff is the absence of an address for the manufacturer or distributor.

WALKABOUT STEREO PLAYERS

Music-on-the-go may be better in theory than in practice. Most lightweight, compact, portable tape players can deliver good sound. Unfortunately, much of that potential goes to waste when you actually walk about with a player. The tiny headphones can't deliver a wide range of sound. (Not that the sound is unpleasant—even mediocre headphones create a "superstereo" effect that often masks sonic defects.)

Furthermore, moving around with a walkabout may increase tape flutter, an unpleasant wavering of sound caused by fluctuations in tape speed. A unit with a snug belt clip is likely to jiggle the least, and so produce the least flutter.

A built-in radio may also not work as well as you'd like. A walkabout uses the headphone's wire as a radio antenna. Moving around may cause the program (especially FM stereo) to fade in and out. Even when you're sitting down, you may have to adjust the wire for best reception.

Convenience. Most walkabouts come with a handy belt clip. A walkabout with a shoulder strap may jiggle too much. Other features to look for:

• *Control position.* It's best to have the tape and tuner controls on top, so you can look down on them when the unit is clipped to your belt.

• *Tape controls.* A number of units reverse automatically at the end of a tape. A light that tells you the tape is running helps remind you to turn off the player when you take off the headphones. An automatic stop after rewind not only means one less button to press, but it also helps preseve the batteries.

• *Tone and volume controls.* An equalizer lets you adjust different bands of the music spectrum, but it doesn't have much of an edge over conventional tone controls.

• *Tape-head cleaning.* The tape head should be at the hinge side of the tape hatch. That makes it easy to reach the head for cleaning.

Loudness. It's possible to play some walkabouts loud enough to endanger hearing. Consider that risk before turning up the volume enough to block out loud outside noises such as a lawn mower.

Think twice about jogging, cycling, or driving with a walkabout playing loud enough to drown out car horns or sirens. In many communities, it's against the law to wear headphones if you're behind the wheel or trotting down the road.

★ 5 ★

Keeping Healthy

AIR CLEANERS

If you can tolerate some chill, fresh air is still the best air cleaner. With an outside temperature of 20°F and a temperature of 70° inside, opening a window a couple of inches costs no more than a few cents an hour in lost heat.

That doesn't make an air-cleaning appliance useless, however. Airborne dust causes many people to sneeze, wheeze, and have other allergic reactions. A good air cleaner, especially if it's used during sleep, can help reduce allergic reaction to dust.

An air cleaner can catch dust more easily than smoke. Dust particles are much larger, and they don't remain airborne for long. However, an air cleaner removes dust only when the particles are in the air, so it won't eliminate dusting and vacuuming.

An air cleaner can also help those allergic to mold spores. For pollen allergies, however, an air conditioner is better. Unlike dust and mold spores, pollen originates outside the house, generally in warm weather when windows are open. An air conditioner circulates air without introducing pollen.

Fan/filter systems. Most air cleaners use a fan to draw the air through a filter. The ability of fans to move air efficiently varies with the model you choose.

Filters vary, too. Granular materials (activated carbon and/or silica gel) are commonly used in inexpensive air cleaners, often in quantities too small to have much of an effect.

Another type of filter is made up of a web of synthetic or glass fiber. It works like a strainer, catching particles that pass through it. This type of fibrous filter can be made more efficient by increasing its surface area—typically by folding it into pleats. A "high-efficiency particulate air filter," or "HEPA filter," pleated and made of glass fibers, is found in a number of home air cleaners.

Still another way to increase the efficiency of a fibrous filter is to include fibers with an electrical charge: the "electret" filter. Many particles in the air have a weak electrical charge, especially in winter. An electret filter catches small charged particles that would otherwise pass through.

Electrostatic precipitator. An air cleaner of this design draws in air with a fan, moving it past an electrode that gives airborne particles an electrical charge. The air then passes a bank of collector plates with opposite electrical charges that trap the dust and other charged particles.

An electrostatic precipitator can be purchased as a component that can be built into a forced-air heating system (a method worth considering if you want to clean the air in an entire house). There are also room-sized electrostatic precipitators similar in size to (or smaller than) a room air conditioner.

Negative-ion generator. Newly designed units can be highly effective at removing smoke, without emitting the toxic ozone that was a problem with some designs of a generation ago. A negative-ion generator spews electrons into the air, turning air molecules into negative ions that seem to give airborne particles a negative charge. The particles then drift to grounded surfaces such as walls and ceilings where they stick, along with smoke particles. This method can stain walls and requires more frequent cleaning of the unit than do other types of air cleaner.

ALLERGY

The symptoms of allergies can range from annoying to life-threatening. Most allergy sufferers have hay fever, or "allergic rhinitis." Less common problems include asthma, skin diseases such as eczema, and food allergies.

The most effective way to treat an allergy is simply to avoid what causes it. Allergists always recommend avoidance before trying other treatments. If your cat or dog makes you wheeze, for example, no treatment can rival the effect of giving the pet away, painful as that may be. If you react to house dust, removing bedroom rugs and putting mattresses and pillows in airtight cases may ease the problem. A dehumidifier can help rid damp areas of mold, another common allergen.

However, avoidance isn't easy with pollen, which causes hay fever and is carried widely in the air. And it may be impossible with other allergens. In such cases, the next-best solution is medication that relieves the symptoms.

Allergy shots. When drugs fall short, you may be a candidate for allergy shots. These shots are effective against some allergens you inhale, such as pollens, and against allergies to insect stings. Once the cause of your allergy is identified, treatment usually begins with shots once or twice a week, with each shot containing an increasingly concentrated dose. Eventually, you reach a maintenance dose. The process commonly takes from four to six months. After that, you should probably receive monthly injections, for at least two years.

Allergy shots can work well, but there is always the danger of an allergic reaction—in very rare cases, severe ones. Before resorting to shots, your doctor should first determine:

- If you've had the symptoms for at least two years—long enough to indicate a chronic problem.
- If the symptoms disrupt your life.
- If avoidance of the allergen and medications don't work.
- If there is evidence that shots will be effective against your particular allergies.

BACK PAIN

If you suffer from an aching back, note that 70 percent of all low-back problems get better in three weeks or less without medical aid, and 90 percent get better, without help, within two months. If you go to a doctor soon after the pain begins, you'll probably be told to take a mild painkiller and go to bed. You'll also be advised to use a firm mattress for better support, or to insert a bed board between a soft mattress and the box spring.

Old-fashioned doctors may also tell you to apply heat in the form of a heating pad, hot baths, or a hot-water bottle. But the latest medical word is that, although mild heat may relax tense muscles and ease muscle spasms, too much heat may make the spasms worse. Excessive heat can also cause burns. Cold compresses or ice packs avoid such problems and decrease pain and spasms more effectively by numbing the area somewhat. Liniments and plasters don't help at all and can cause burns if used with a heating pad.

There is no fixed limit on how long to stay in bed. Doctors used to recommend as much as two weeks of uninterrupted bed rest, but two days may be just as effective. You should get out of bed when you *can* get out, even if your back still hurts somewhat. Staying longer in bed won't speed up your recovery.

Don't leave your bed and move to a chair. Sitting puts much more strain on an aching back than does walking. Standing in one position also increases back strain.

When to see a physician. Sometimes the pain doesn't let up, even after bed rest. These symptoms suggest that your pain may require professional help:

- Pain that lasts more than a week or two and worsens despite bed rest.
- Pain so bad that it wakes you up at night or prevents you from functioning.
- Pain that doesn't ease when you shift your posture—especially when you lie down.
- Pain that shoots down a leg.
- Numbness or weakness of a leg or foot.
- Loss of control over bladder or bowels.
- Pain associated with a specific trauma, such as a fall or an auto injury.
- Pain accompanied by fever, nausea, vomiting, urinary discomfort, general weakness, or sweating.

Even in the absence of those symptoms, medical assistance is appropriate if you are worried about the pain. Consult a doctor, too, when back pain occurs in an elderly person or a child.

BLOOD-PRESSURE MONITORS

If you have been diagnosed as hypertensive and are under a physician's care, a blood-pressure monitor is a good investment. It's a device that will help you collaborate with the doctor in your treatment. Readings taken at home tend to be trustworthy, if only because you won't have the anxiety many people experience in the doctor's office. *Note:* Don't use a blood-pressure monitor to make a diagnosis for yourself or anyone else, and don't let a series of normal readings persuade you to alter or stop medication without first talking to your physician. In fact, it's a good idea to bring your monitor along the next time you visit the doctor, so your technique with the device can be checked.

Electronic models whose cuffs inflate automatically are the simplest to operate: You put on the cuff, position it, press a button, and read your pressure on a digital display. However, an electronic machine won't hit your "true" pressure on the nose. Many will be in error by 5 points (millimeters of mercury) or more, at least occasionally. These types of monitors are best for checking a trend over weeks or months. Electronic machines also can be in error for medical reasons, depending on the patient. If you get frequent error messages, return the device: It's not working properly for you.

As a group, *mechanical* monitors are often more accurate than the electronic units. But a mechanical blood-pressure monitor requires dexterity, good hearing (you must use a stethoscope), good eyesight (you must read a dial), some training, and a bit of practice. Otherwise you might wind up making errors worse than the monitor's inherent range of error.

BRITTLE NAILS

Weak or brittle fingernails aren't usually a sign of disease. The problem is often caused by frequent or prolonged exposure to water. Wet nails swell; drying makes them shrink. Repeated swell-dry cycles tend to cause nail ends to break and split. Swimmers, cooks, homemakers, and bartenders often complain of brittle nails.

A diet that's severely deficient in protein or calories will weaken you and your nails. However, no specific food or nutrient will strengthen nails or prevent them from breaking. Gelatin, calcium, or vitamin supplements won't help.

Some tips for stronger nails:

• Minimize contact with water. If possible, use rubber gloves when washing dishes or otherwise dealing with water.

• Avoid nail polish removers containing acetone, which tends to dry out nails.

• Nail hardeners may offer temporary relief, but they have to be reapplied at regular intervals.

GENERIC DRUGS

Want to save money on prescriptions? Avoid brand-name drugs. Prescription drugs marketed under their generic names often are half the price of the same drug sold under a brand name—that is, the name given it by the company that held the original patent.

Most generic drugs are not manufactured by fly-by-night factories but by the same companies that develop brand-name drugs. In fact, 60-odd brand-name drug companies make about 80 percent of generic drugs too. Some 300 smaller pharmaceutical companies produce the drugs for the rest of the generic market.

If you want to realize the savings offered by generic drugs, you will need the cooperation of both your doctor and your pharmacist. Doctors, for instance, usually write the brand name when they prescribe; it's shorter and easier to remember than the generic name.

That medical habit doesn't prevent you from buying generically. The laws in every state allow pharmacists to substitute a less-expensive generic version even when a doctor prescribes by brand. Indeed, the doctor must make a conscious effort to limit you to the brand name—in some states, by writing "dispense as written" or some other phrase on the prescription. In other states, the doctor must sign a line on the prescription form that indicates if the patient must receive the specified brand or if the pharmacist may substitute a generic.

If you switch from a brand name to a generic, the medication's color and shape will be different from the brand-name product you've been taking. The pill's appearance won't affect how the drug works. However, some patients may become confused about medications whose color or shape changes, particularly if they usually transfer a day's worth of pills from the prescription vial to a pocket or purse container. An unfamiliar appearance could promote taking the wrong pill at the wrong time and/ or in the wrong amount. In such instances, prudence suggests sticking to a brand-name drug, even if more expensive. After all, peace of mind has a value, too.

HEALTH INFORMATION

The government's National Health Information Clearinghouse will respond to your health questions. NHIC forwards your questions to one or more of the many health-related organizations listed in its database.

To contact the NHIC, call 800-336-4797 or, in Virginia, 703-522-2590.

You can also contact some of NHIC's referral organizations directly. Here are a few of them:

- Alzheimer's Disease and Related Disorders Association. 800-621-0379; 800-572-6037 in Illinois.
- National Asthma Center. 800-222-LUNG; 303-398-1477 in Colorado.
- National Cocaine Hotline. 800-COC-AINE.
- National Abortion Federation. 800-772-9100; 202-546-9060 in Washington, D.C.
- Pregnancy Crisis Center. 800-368-3336; 804-847-6828 (call collect within Virginia).
- National Parkinson Foundation. 800-327-4545; 800-433-7022 in Florida; 305-547-6666 in Miami.
- National Second Surgical Opinion Program Hotline. 800-638-6833; 800-492-6603 in Maryland.
- VD National Hotline. 800-227-8922; 800-982-5883 in California.

IMMUNIZATION FOR ADULTS

Antidisease shots aren't just for kids. The U.S. Centers for Disease Control and the American College of Physicians recommend six vaccines for routine use in adults:

Tetanus/diphtheria toxoid. Most adults probably don't have adequate protection against these two potentially fatal diseases. Everyone should obtain a booster shot every 10 years.

Rubella vaccine. Rubella, or German measles, is usually a mild disease in adults. But its effect on a developing fetus can be devastating, producing blindness or other birth defects. The vaccine is recommended for adults who have not previously had rubella or a rubella immunization, especially women of childbearing age. Women who intend to become pregnant should check their immunization status. But vaccination for rubella during pregnancy should be avoided.

Measles vaccine. Anyone born after 1956 who did not receive live measles vaccine after one year of age should be immunized (unless there's a reliable record of prior infection or laboratory evidence of immunity).

Influenza vaccine. An annual flu shot is recommended for anyone at high risk for influenza. That group takes in anyone over 65 and adults or children with chronic illnesses, including heart, lung, kidney, or metabolic disorders (such as diabetes and cystic fibrosis), chronic anemia, or an impaired immune-defense system.

Pneumococcal vaccine. A single, one-time injection is advised for all older adults, especially those over 65. It's also recommended for patients of any age with chronic heart or lung disease, diabetes, alcoholism, cirrhosis of the liver, Hodgkin's disease, disorders of the spleen, kidney disease, multiple myeloma, cerebrospinal-fluid leaks, sickle-cell anemia, and impaired immune defenses.

Hepatitis B vaccine. Immunization against hepatitis B infection, which can cause severe, chronic liver disease, is recommended for people in certain high-risk groups: household and sexual contacts of hepatitis-B carriers, male homosexuals, intravenous drug users, patients and staff of institutions for the mentally retarded, dialysis patients, hemophiliacs, health workers, mortuary staff, and others who are frequently exposed to blood or blood products.

The vaccine is expensive, and previous exposure to the virus may not have been recognized, so it may be worthwhile to submit a blood specimen for testing. If hepatitis-B antibodies are present, no vaccination is necessary.

INSOMNIA

Occasional sleeplessness doesn't make you a confirmed insomniac. Insomnia has three forms: *Transient* insomnia occurs among normal sleepers who suffer a few restless nights because of jet lag, trouble at the office, or various anxiety-provoking or exciting events. *Short-term* insomnia can come from more serious stress such as job loss, fear of serious illness, or a death in the family. *Chronic* insomnia may go on for months or years with no obvious explanation. It may be a symptom of persistent depression, or it might occur with overuse of sleep medication, too much alcohol, or disturbances of one's "biological clock" (as with someone whose job hours shift).

Various drugs can promote insomnia. Stimulants such as caffeine and appetite suppressants are well-known offenders. Some drugs prescribed for insomnia can interfere with normal sleep patterns. Worry about insomnia can also make insomnia worse.

To counter sleep-robbing habits:

● Establish a fixed sleep schedule. Go to bed and get up at set times. Don't try to make up for lost sleep on weekends and holidays.

● Stop napping, day or evening.

● Never stay in bed when you can't sleep. Do something relaxing—read, listen to music, watch television—until you're sleepy.

● Exercise regularly, preferably in the morning or well before dinner.

● Avoid caffeine in the late afternoon or evening.

● Eat at the same time each day. Try to plan relaxing evening activities, including light exercise such as a leisurely walk.

● Minimize external distractions at bedtime. For example, use dark window shades or eye coverings to block out annoying light.

If insomnia persists despite sleep-hygiene measures, it's time for professional help. An internist or other primary-care physician is a good first choice. A caring physician will spend time taking a thorough medical history, including a sleep history. Depending on the problem, the prescription may range from a full-scale medical exam to a short course of medication or referral to a sleep clinic.

PAIN RELIEVERS

There are only three types of pain reliever available without a doctor's prescription: those containing aspirin, acetaminophen, or ibuprofen. For most people, occasional use of any of the three is quite safe. But each can cause side effects in certain individuals.

Aspirin has remained popular because it works. Two 325-milligram (5 grain) tablets at four-hour intervals will relieve mild-to-moderate pain and reduce fever. Aspirin's action against inflammation makes it important in treating arthritis.

Aspirin can irritate the stomach, however. Heavy users, such as arthritics, face an increased risk of serious stomach bleeding. Aspirin also inhibits blood clotting, a characteristic that has led some doctors to suggest aspirin for people who have had heart attack or stroke warnings.

Don't count on buffered aspirin's being faster-acting or more soothing to the stomach than plain aspirin. Enteric-coated aspirin does cause less stomach irritation; the tablets' coating keeps them from dissolving until they reach the small intestine.

Certain individuals, often those with severe asthma or chronic hives, are aspirin-sensitive and must avoid aspirin. So should anyone with ulcers or other stomach problems, except under a physician's supervision, and pregnant women, especially during the last three months of pregnancy. Children with flu or chicken pox should never be given aspirin, which may cause a rare but often fatal disorder called Reye's syndrome.

Acetaminophen shares aspirin's ability to reduce fever and relieve mild-to-moderate pain, but it lacks aspirin's anti-inflammatory effect. Acetaminophen's main advantage is that it's gentler (but not totally nonirritating) to the stomach than aspirin.

People who drink a lot of alcohol should avoid acetaminophen. They risk liver damage, even with moderate doses.

Ibuprofen, the first new nonprescription analgesic in nearly 35 years, seems to work much like aspirin in the body. Ibuprofen isn't considered as irritating to the stomach as aspirin, but it is more so than acetaminophen.

Large doses of ibuprofen can reduce blood flow to

the kidneys. Those who should take ibuprofen only under a doctor's supervision include people on diuretics and anyone with kidney disease, heart disease, severe hypertension, or cirrhosis of the liver. Elderly people with or without such problems also face a risk, because kidney function declines with age. In general, anyone who should avoid aspirin for any reason should also avoid ibuprofen, and vice versa.

Milligram for milligram, aspirin and acetaminophen are equally potent. Two regular-strength tablets (650 milligrams, or 10 grains) handle most headaches and other minor aches and pains.

Ibuprofen appears to have some advantages over aspirin and acetaminophen. Studies suggest that one 200-milligram tablet relieves pain slightly better than 650 milligrams of either aspirin or acetaminophen. Ibuprofen is especially helpful for treating pain from "soft tissue" injuries such as strains and sprains, pain after dental surgery, and menstrual pain.

SUNSCREENS AND SUNBURN

A tan may be fashionable, but the unpleasant truth is that sunlight damages skin—whether or not you suffer a sunburn. The sun's ultraviolet radiation damages the skin's elastin fibers, causing sagging, wrinkling, and a generally weatherbeaten look. The damage is irreversible and cumulative; signs of overexposure may not show up for 20 or 30 years. Overexposure also causes skin cancer.

Unfortunately, you can't always tell you've had too much sun on any given day until it's too late. Sunburn doesn't appear until about two hours after exposure, and symptoms don't reach their peak for 16 to 24 hours. The darker your complexion, the more natural sunburn protection you have. But even the darkest-skinned people can burn if their exposure is severe enough.

Most of the sun's effect is caused by UV-B ultraviolet radiation. Another type, UV-A, can cause photosensitive skin reactions in people taking certain drugs and may cause cataracts over time.

Short of staying indoors, the best way to protect your skin is to use a sunscreen with a high sun-protection factor (SPF). The SPF indicates a multiple of the time it takes the sun to produce a certain effect on your skin. A person who can stay in the sun for just 30 minutes without burning would be protected for 60 minutes with an SPF 2 sunscreen or for 10 hours with an SPF 20 sunscreen. Most sunscreens are formulated to filter both UV-A and UV-B.

The label on a sunscreen can tell you a lot:

• *Waterproof* means the product will protect you at the labeled SPF value even after four 20-minute swims. A water-resistant product should retain its SPF through two such swims.

• *Clear lotion,* better described as a liquid, is a clear, alcohol-based product that leaves a noticeable film on your skin when it dries. The product isn't greasy: Sand won't stick to it.

• *"Highest level of protection"* may be loosely used. SPF 15 is virtually a total sun block in most of the continental United States, but you can find products with SPFs in the 20s and 30s for use in the tropics.

• *The Skin Cancer Foundation* is a nonprofit educational group whose acceptance seal appears on some sunscreens. The seal indicates a waterproof or water-resistant product with an SPF of at least 15.

• *Sunscreen chemicals* are potent. Many of them, especially PABA (Para-aminobenzoic acid) and PABA derivatives can irritate skin. If a sunscreen makes your skin red or itchy, switch to a brand with different active ingredients.

Tanning. If you're very fair, you need a sunscreen that provides total or near-total protection. People with a light to medium complexion, who burn only moderately and tan to a light brown, can use a sunscreen of SPF 4 to 6. Dark-skinned people can probably use a sunscreen of SPF 2, or no sunscreen at all. As you tan, you can gradually decrease the SPF number on the sunscreen you use.

TANNING SALONS

Tanning salons promote the idea that the equipment they use reduces or eliminates "harmful" ultraviolet-B rays (UV-B), and steps up the output of "safe" ultraviolet-A (UV-A) rays. Both cause the skin to tan, but UV-B is much more apt to cause sunburn.

The American Medical Association has issued a report that warns of many possible dangers from

sunlamps. "Many people, particularly young people, . . . are going to have significant problems,"
said Dr. Paul Lazar, professor of clinical dermatol-
ogy at Northwestern University Medical School and
an author of the AMA report.

Dr. Lazar and other dermatologists are not reas-
sured by tanning salons' switch to UV-A. Sunburn,
they point out, is only one potential danger. UV-A,
which penetrates more deeply into the skin, can
produce the wrinkled, leathery look of prematurely
aged skin. Sunlight, in particular its ultraviolet portion, also induces skin cancer. While UV-B is the
most carcinogenic fraction of the spectrum, some
studies indicate that UV-A can harm the cornea and
lens of the eye; repeated exposure to either UV-A or
UV-B may cause cataracts.

Dr. Lazar noted that UV-B provides a "biological
marker." When you get a sunburn, he said, "you
know you've had enough." But with UV-A, you
don't have any warning signal.

TICK-BORNE DISEASES

In 1976, Dr. Allen Steere of the Yale University
Medical School announced the discovery of a new
disease. He dubbed it "Lyme arthritis," after the
Connecticut town where some children had developed painful arthritic symptoms. The disease is
spread by an adolescent stage of the deer tick called
a "nymph."

In the Northeast, nymphs are active in late spring
and summer, when people tend to be outdoors.
Much smaller than adult ticks, they are hard to spot
on clothing or skin. Most people who contract
Lyme disease have been bitten by nymphs.

Ticks transmit several other diseases, but usually
only in limited areas and relatively infrequently.
Babesiosis produces headache, fever, and chills, in
about a dozen people a year, mainly on Cape Cod,
Massachusetts, and on the eastern end of Long Is-
land in New York State. *Colorado tick fever*, which affects an estimated 50 to 150 people annually, occurs
only among those who live or work at altitudes
above 4,000 feet.

An exception to the localized pattern is *Rocky
Mountain spotted fever*, which was reported in 40
states in 1986. Of 775 recent cases, nearly half oc-
curred in the Southeast. Rocky Mountain spotted

fever can be fatal. The infecting microbe is transmitted by the Rocky Mountain wood tick in the West and the American dog tick in the East.

Nearly all cases of Rocky Mountain spotted fever occur in spring and summer, generally several days after exposure to infected ticks. The onset of illness is abrupt, often with high fever, headache, chills, and severe weakness. By about the fourth day of fever, victims develop a spotted pink rash, which usually starts on the hands and feet and gradually extends to most of the body. As with Lyme disease, early detection and treatment significantly reduce the severity of the illness.

Prevention. In areas of tick-borne disease:

• Don't go out barefoot or in open sandals. Wear long pants, cinched at the ankle or tucked into boots or socks for added protection.

• Wear light-colored clothing outdoors to make ticks easier to spot. Check your clothes every so often. Be especially careful in terrain with tall grass, bushes, or woods. Try to stay in the middle of trails to avoid contact with tick-bearing bushes.

• Use a tick repellent if you spend a lot of time outdoors.

• With children, start a bedtime check for ticks from mid-April through September.

• Check pets for ticks.

• Know what to look for. A biting deer tick rarely hurts enough to draw your attention. To find one you'll have to look for it—especially the tiny nymph, which is smaller than a sesame seed. A nymph that's been attached to the skin for several hours looks like a blood blister with legs.

• Pregnant women should be especially careful— Lyme-disease spirochetes can cross the placenta.

TOOTHPASTES

Plaque is a soft, sticky bacterial film that coats teeth. If sufficient plaque accumulates and grows down into the crevices between teeth and gums, gum disease may result. Plaque that isn't brushed away can combine with minerals in saliva to form a calcified plaque called *tartar* or *calculus*. Tartar is a rock-hard, white or yellowish deposit that can only be "scaled" from teeth and from under gums during professional cleaning.

Regular, thorough brushing and flossing can re-move almost all plaque—and tartar as well. Tartar collects mainly on the tooth surfaces most exposed to saliva. Extra brushing near the salivary glands (the tongue side of the lower front teeth and the cheek side of the upper back teeth) can prevent most tartar buildup.

Toothpastes that make antitartar claims do con-tain effective antitartar ingredients. Unfortunately, they'll do nothing to dissolve tartar that's already on your teeth. Further, they inhibit tartar only above the gum line, not where a toothbrush doesn't reach, so they do little for dental health.

To help remove plaque and stains, all toothpastes contain abrasives such as hydrated silica or phos-phate salts. Toothpaste won't affect tooth enamel, the visible part of a tooth. But when gums recede with age or disease, softer dental tissues become ex-posed that can be damaged by a toothpaste that's too abrasive.

Use the least abrasive toothpaste that gets your teeth clean, especially if your gums have begun to recede. People with heavily stained teeth may re-quire a more abrasive toothpaste, at least occasionally.

Another important factor in choosing a tooth-paste is fluoride. A fluoride formula that has been shown to be effective can give everyone, regardless of age, added protection against cavities.

The American Dental Association (ADA) has a Council on Dental Therapeutics that requires man-ufacturers to submit rigorous research data demon-strating that the fluoride in a toothpaste actually works in preventing tooth decay.

★ 6 ★

Food and Nutrition

BABY NUTRITION

For their first six months of life, most babies get all the nutrients they need from breast milk or formula. In fact, their digestive systems aren't mature enough to handle other foods. Babies may even push food out of their mouths with their tongues, a reflex that protects them from substances they can't properly swallow or digest. Some studies suggest that introducing solids to infants younger than six months just adds needless calories, since the baby will still drink the same amount of milk.

Somewhere around four to six months, babies develop the neuromuscular mechanisms they need to swallow solids. They also begin to grow too hungry to be satisfied by milk alone. But every baby is different, so starting an infant on solids should be determined by a baby's readiness, not merely by weight or age.

How to start. Pediatricians usually recommend starting with infant cereals, which are fortified with vitamins and minerals (particularly iron) that complement the baby's diet of breast milk or formula. Introduce other solid foods one at a time, at intervals of a week or so. It will then be much easier to identify any food intolerances, which might show up as loose bowel movements, rashes, or other allergic reactions.

Each new food presents a new taste and texture experience for a child. So offer the food in small amounts. Don't worry if you get more on the baby than into his or her mouth. By about one year of age, baby's digestive processes should be functioning at nearly an adult level, so most foods can come from the family table.

Some other tips:

• Don't feed the baby straight from the original jar or a storage container, lest bacteria from the baby's mouth be transferred from the spoon and contaminate the jar. Instead, spoon what you need into a bowl, then cover the remainder and store it in the refrigerator for no more than a few days.

• Rarely are there significant differences in nutrition or price among commercial infant and junior foods. You may want to avoid those few products that contain added sugars, salt, or modified starches. Read the labels to find out which foods contain these additives.

CEREALS, READY-TO-EAT

As nature makes them, cereal grains are naturally low in fat, sodium, and sugar. But that's not true of many ready-to-eat cereals. In a serving of some packaged cereals, you eat the equivalent in fat of a pat of butter, or more. In others, you get a dose of sodium rivaling that found in some salty snack foods. In still others, half the cereal is sugar.

Cereal grains are "nutrient dense"—for their calories, they deliver good food value that includes complex carbohydrates (starches), fiber, B vitamins, and protein. In ready-to-eat cereals, though, manufacturing removes some nutrients. Manufacturers do restore lost nutrients, but sometimes not to your benefit. They can and do add fat, sodium, and sugar, never to your benefit.

Much of the information you need to make an informed choice of a cereal is right on the label:

Fiber. Although some ready-to-eat cereals make fiber an important selling point, manufacturers aren't required to disclose fiber content, and few do—probably because so many cereals are short on fiber. Anyway, you should think of fiber as part of your overall diet, not just as a morning "dose" of cereal.

Protein. The protein in grain is not what nutritionists term "complete." Unlike the protein in meat or fish, cereal protein lacks certain essential amino acids, which are protein's building blocks. However, cereals "borrow" nutrients to complete their protein from the milk you add to your bowl.

Sugar. Manufacturers add several kinds: table sugar (sucrose), corn syrup, honey, and the like. The less sugar, the better—sugar can promote cavities by providing a feast for decay-causing oral bacteria. That's especially true when a sugary cereal is eaten dry, as a snack. The added sugars, unlike the sugars you may add yourself in the form of bananas or blueberries, are also "empty calories" that provide no useful nutrients apart from their food energy.

Sodium. Many cereal manufacturers routinely add salt. That's no favor to people with hypertension who must limit their salt intake. Reducing sodium intake may also benefit the 20 percent or so of the general population that's susceptible to high blood pressure.

Calories. Cereals are fairly low in calories—usually about 110 an ounce. (A half cup of whole milk adds 75 calories; low-fat milk, 43 calories.) Some higher-fat brands, though, contain substantially more calories. If you are counting calories, watch out for the amount of cereal you use. Cereals have various densities: A bowl that holds exactly an ounce by weight of one brand will hold $3\frac{1}{2}$ ounces of a denser cereal, thus more than tripling the calories.

FAST FOOD

If you're after good nutrition, don't eat typical fast food often. A steady diet of the usual fast-food items will overload you with protein, fat, and calories while shortchanging you on minerals and fiber. To balance a meal of burger, shake, and fries, you'd have to search out low-fat, vitamin- and mineral-rich fare for the rest of the day.

However, you *can* put together a fairly well-balanced meal by choosing from a fast-food menu wisely. Here's how:

• Choose roast beef over hamburgers if you can; roast beef is often leaner. Add tomato, lettuce, and such to enhance the meal with extra nutrients.

• Choose small, plain hamburgers instead of the

giant, mouth-filling variety with the works. Skip the mayonnaise, to save about 150 calories, and avoid cheese, whose protein and calcium come with fat.

• Choose regular fried chicken, not the "extra crispy" kind. Extra fat adds the crispiness and probably 100 calories or so per piece.

• Order milk instead of a shake. Low-fat milk provides much more protein and calcium per calorie than a fast-food shake. Or order a diet soda.

• If you want to cut calories, go easy on french fried potatoes. Split an order with someone else or order a plain baked potato instead, if available.

• Choose a fast-food salad. A boxed salad with chicken or shrimp will supply some protein along with the fiber, complex carbohydrates, vitamins, and minerals from the vegetables. At a salad bar, choose carrots, tomatoes, and dark green vegetables. Go easy on dressings, fatty croutons, taco chips, and mayonnaise-laden pasta and potato salads.

HOT DOGS

Americans love hot dogs—they wolf down some 19 billion each year. But hot dogs consist largely of water and fat. Odds and ends of meat ground with water and spices are pumped into casings, cooked, cured, and packaged. Currently the U.S. Department of Agriculture (USDA) allows manufacturers to add up to 10 percent more water than is normally found in meat. This water is mostly in the form of ice, meant to keep the meat cool while it is being ground.

The USDA also allows manufacturers to make hot dogs with up to 30 percent fat, the amount found in a well-marbled steak. With so much water and fat, there's not much room for protein in a hot dog—it only averages 13 percent, while cooked steak and hamburger are almost 25 percent protein by weight. That means you can pay more for a pound of protein in a hot dog than you would for a pound of protein in a sirloin steak.

Spices and preservatives. Processors can also add up to 3.5 percent nonmeat and nonwater ingredients, which are usually binders, such as skim milk. Preservatives and flavorings are also added, such as salt, sweeteners such as corn syrup or dextrose, ascorbic acid (vitamin C) or one of its derivatives, such as sodium erythorbate or sodium ascorbate, and nitrite.

Nitrite is by far the more controversial. It preserves meat and gives it its characteristic flavor and color; it also inhibits the growth of the bacterium that causes botulism, a form of food poisoning that's often fatal. The controversy centers on whether nitrite poses a cancer hazard in the quantities consumed. The Food and Drug Administration and the USDA have permitted the use of lowered amounts of nitrite but have not banned it, mainly because no substitute has been developed that matches its preservative effects. Many scientists also consider any risks posed by nitrite to be minimal and preferable to the risks of doing without it in cured meats.

Most hot dogs are high in sodium as well: a good-tasting wiener may contain 400 milligrams or more of sodium.

Obviously, hot dogs do not bring joy to the heart of a nutritionist or a prudent dieter. But if you insist on eating them occasionally, buy the tastiest you can and enjoy them. On an ideal hot dog, the outer "skin" should resist slightly when you bite into it. Breaking through this outer layer, you should be rewarded with a spurt of meaty juice. The meat at the center should be moist and firm.

MAIL-ORDER FOOD

The high prices charged by mail-order food companies often buy you fancy packaging and trimmings. But do fancy prices buy better quality than you can get from a local store?

Filet mignon. The best mail-order steaks are tender and flavorful, with no off-flavors or visible fat or gristle. But not every steak-by-mail's a superior product. Before ordering, check out a local butcher shop. Prime filet mignon could turn out to be as good as the best mail-order steak, and a lot less expensive.

Smoked salmon. If you're buying mail-order salmon as a gift, don't expect top quality. Buy the least expensive brand you can, and hope the fancy wrapping pleases the recipient enough to compensate for what's inside. If you're buying for yourself, you may get better salmon by shopping around the corner.

Cheddar cheese. You may find fresh cheddar locally that's as good as the best you can get by mail. Look for cheese that's creamy yellow, with no color change or dryness at the edges. There should be a slight crumbliness at the cut edge, and the cheese should be wrapped tightly.

Coffee beans. Coffee beans are an ideal mail-order food. They require no special packaging or handling, and they're not heavy. An unusual variety of coffee can be a nice present for someone who doesn't have a specialty shop nearby. And it can be fun to buy for yourself, since you can experiment with various types that may not be available in your area.

In most cases, it should take a week or two for a mail-order company to deliver your order. If the package spoils during shipping or you or the person you sent it to is not satisfied when it arrives, most mail-order companies will refund your money or re-ship the order.

MICROWAVE CAKE BAKING

Cake mixes intended for baking in a microwave oven can be improved by a few simple changes in the recipe. These changes can also work with conventional cake mixes that are baked in a microwave oven.

Here's what to do:

• Mix the batter with an electric mixer until it is completely smooth. That gives the cake a better "crumb," or texture.

• Line the bottom of the baking pan with a circle of waxed paper, and put another circle on top of the batter. That prevents a skin from forming on the cake.

• To bake the cake, set it in its pan on an inverted dinner plate in the oven. That helps bake the cake evenly.

• Begin by baking on a low wattage (power level), such as the Defrost setting; use five minutes with a light-colored cake, a couple of minutes longer with a chocolate cake. Then rotate the cake half a turn and bake it on High (full power) for $1\frac{1}{2}$ to 2 minutes. Finally, rotate the cake again and bake it another $1\frac{1}{2}$ to 2 minutes, again on High.

ORANGE JUICE

A morning glass of orange juice is a good way to meet your need for vitamin C. On average, a six-ounce serving of juice from frozen concentrate provides an adult's Recommended Daily Allowance of 60 milligrams of vitamin C.

Orange juice is also a good source of potassium, as are many other common foods, such as meat, potatoes, bananas, and peanut butter. Since potassium is so abundant, healthy people rarely, if ever, develop a potassium deficiency. (Indeed, there is no Recommended Daily Allowance for potassium. Typical daily intakes range from 800 to 5,000 milligrams.) A six-ounce serving of orange juice contains about 350 milligrams. People who take potassium-depleting medication (some drugs used for treating hypertension, for example) may need extra potassium. That's something to discuss with your doctor.

Orange juice is nutritious, but it's not a diet drink. Ounce for ounce, it has about as many calories as cola or beer: roughly 80 calories per six-ounce serving. More than 10 percent of orange juice is fruit sugar. That's why people on a diet are advised to eat an orange rather than drink a glassful of juice, the equivalent of three or four oranges.

Orange juice packaged in a box (not to be confused with chilled juice in the dairy case) is heated, quickly cooled, then packed in multilayer cartons without any air space. This packaging is called "aseptic." Like cans, aseptic cartons can be stored at room temperature and packed in a lunchbox or bought from a vending machine without fear of spoilage.

Its taste, however, leaves a great deal to be desired. Consider boxed juice only for situations in which convenience and portability compensate for poor flavor. The taste is just about on a par with canned juice, and often has the same metallic off-flavor.

Fresh-squeezed juices aside, the best-tasting orange juices are frozen concentrates and chilled juices. The frozen variety tastes better—assuming that your tap water also tastes good—and often costs less.

If frozen and chilled juice aren't stored in an airtight jar, their flavor and the vitamin C content deteriorate. If you like the convenience of chilled juice, consider buying it by the quart to preserve freshness, rather than in the two-quart size.

SWEETENERS

Switching to an artificial sweetener may not help you to control your weight—you're apt to eat more food, leaving total calorie intake unchanged or even increased. Still, if you can't stand unsweetened food, here's a rundown on your options:

Sugar. Sucrose, corn sweeteners (such as corn syrup), and other sugars are equivalent in calories. A teaspoon of sugar contains 16 calories, a can of sugar-sweetened soda, about 160. If you're dieting, fat is an even greater source of calories. Fats contain 9 calories per gram, compared with 4 for sugar and other carbohydrates.

Sugar that clings to the teeth—in candy, honey, and the like—is more likely to promote tooth decay than are sugared liquids such as beverages.

Saccharin. This calorie-free compound, 300 times sweeter than sugar, promotes cancer in laboratory animals. The sole U.S. maker of saccharin notes that people have been using saccharin for almost a century with no clear indication of ill effects. However, that doesn't necessarily mean that saccharin is safe.

Aspartame. Aspartame has the same number of calories as sugar, weight for weight. However, it is 200 times sweeter than sugar, so it contributes only 1/200th as many calories to the diet. Some aspartame products use glucose, a sugar, as a carrier. That adds a few calories, but the total remains lower than in an equivalent portion of sugar.

Some questions remain about aspartame's safety, but it seems to be acceptably safe for most people when used in moderation. However, aspartame may be a problem for people who suffer from a metabolic disorder called phenylketonuria (PKU). Their bodies lack an enzyme to process phenylalanine, an amino acid that's one of aspartame's two components. Accordingly, the chemical can build up to toxic levels in their blood and tissues. Even for PKU patients, however, aspartame has been judged to pose only a small risk.

Sorbitol. This sweetener (and its close relative, mannitol) is used in sugar-free candies, mints, chewing gum, and the like. Sorbitol is found naturally in some fruits and berries. It has the same number of calories per gram as ordinary table sugar, but it's only about half as sweet. Unlike sugar, however, sorbitol does not promote dental cavities.

Sorbitol is digested slowly, so it's used in some ''low sugar'' gums and candies for diabetics. Some people are troubled by excess gas when consuming sorbitol or mannitol.

TURKEY

Fond of turkey? Here's how to get the best from a bird:

Cook a turkey uncovered, breast up, in a 325° oven, to an internal temperature of 185°. Use a meat thermometer—neither tugging on a drumstick to see if it lifts easily away from the body nor watching the pop-up thermometer included with many turkeys is a reliable method of temperature control.

If you try to make a turkey juicier by covering it and letting it cook in its own juices, you lose some of the complex flavors that come from roasting. Instead, try basting, oiling the breast before roasting, or covering the breast with aluminum foil. Or cut off the neck skin near the neck cavity and stretch it over the breast, securing it with toothpicks.

Turkey is low in calories and saturated fat. If you're watching your fat intake, you may want to avoid dark meat. It's about twice as fatty as white meat (though still fairly lean compared with other meats). Avoid eating the skin—ounce for ounce, it has about 12 times as much fat as white meat. You can also avoid fat by using a gravy jug with a spout rising from the base. When you tip the jug, you pour the protein-rich gravy out from under the floating fat.

Most frozen turkeys have been injected with a prebasting solution made up of fats, salt, phosphates, flavoring, broth, and water. The solution is supposed to enhance juiciness, but it doesn't do very much. Fortunately, much of the fat ends up in the drip pan.

Some frozen turkeys also contain monosodium glutamate (MSG), which adds sodium and may cause allergic reactions. If you are sensitive to MSG, check the ingredients list carefully.

Food poisoning. Take a few simple precautions:

• A frozen turkey starts thawing rather fast, particularly on a warm day or in a heated car. Take it straight home to the freezer.

• Wash your hands before handling food. Wear gloves if you have cuts, abrasions, or skin infections. Rinse raw turkey with cold water, to wash bacteria from the surface. Then scrub your hands, utensils, and all work surfaces with soap and hot water.

• Thaw turkey on a tray in the refrigerator. An eight-pound bird will thaw in about a day. Allow an extra day for every additional four pounds.

For quick thawing, put the turkey in a watertight plastic bag, set it in a large bowl or a clean sink, and cover it with cold (not warm!) water. Change the water every half hour. An 8-pound bird should thaw in about 4 hours; a 24-pound bird, in about 12 hours. Or use a microwave oven for thawing, if it's big enough.

• You can't judge doneness by color. In young turkeys, for example, red color from the marrow can seep into the meat, making the legs and thighs look red and undercooked even when they're done.

• Don't get attached to turkey leftovers. Eat what you can in two or three days, then freeze what's left or throw it away.

TURKEY ROLLS

Love turkey but hate to deal with it? Turkey rolls and roasts look appealing for their easy preparation—no thawing, basting, stuffing, or disguising the leftovers. But they are not very good. These rolls can be gristly, salty, oily, and wet (instead of juicy). They may also taste heavily of broth and processing, without much turkey flavor. And turkey rolls are much more expensive, pound for pound, than whole turkeys.

A serving of turkey roll contains about the same

calories as a serving of turkey breast. But the roll derives fewer of those calories from protein and more from fat. The rolls also contain a lot of sodium, about 600 milligrams in a $3\frac{1}{2}$-ounce serving. Turkey breast, by contrast, contains about a third as much sodium.

VITAMIN SUPPLEMENTS

It's possible to overdose on some vitamins. The body doesn't get rid of fat-soluble vitamins efficiently; they're generally stored until they can be used up. Prolonged, excessive intake of vitamin A can cause headache, increased pressure on the brain, bone pain, and damage to the liver. Too much vitamin D can cause kidney damage.

Water-soluble vitamins are generally excreted quickly when taken to excess, but some can still cause trouble. Large doses of niacin can cause liver damage, severe flushes, and skin rash. High doses of vitamin C can cause diarrhea. Too much vitamin B$_6$ over long periods can damage the nervous system.

Don't take vitamins for "insurance"—the best way to get them is from a balanced diet. Evaluate your diet to see if you're eating a variety of foods from the Basic Four groups. If you have trouble figuring that out, record what you eat for a week and check with a registered dietician or a physician. If you are missing anything, improve your eating habits. Avoid doctors or nutrition consultants who recommend vitamins as cure-alls.

Vitamin supplementation may be appropriate for children up to two years old or with poor eating habits, for some people on prolonged weight-reduction programs, for pregnant women, for strict vegetarians, and for people with certain illnesses, as directed by a physician. As a rule, those people shouldn't take more than the RDA amounts (the Recommended Dietary Allowances published by the Food and Nutrition Board of the National Research Council/National Academy of Sciences).

Minerals. You may, however, need more of certain minerals than you get from your diet. Here are three minerals that some people should pay special attention to:

• *Fluoride* taken in childhood helps build decay-resistant teeth. The most efficient, economical way to get it is through fluoridated water. Children who grow up in nonfluoridated communities should take supplemental fluoride (by prescription) from birth through age 12.

• *Calcium* intake, if inadequate, is a factor in the development of osteoporosis (thinning of the bones), especially in women. If you like milk, cheese, and other dairy products, you may get enough from diet alone. If you don't eat much calcium-rich food, ask a doctor or registered dietician about supplementation.

• *Iron* is needed to make hemoglobin, the component in red blood cells that carries oxygen to the tissues. Lack of sufficient iron causes iron-deficiency anemia. Women who are pregnant or who menstruate heavily should be checked by a doctor to be sure they are not anemic.

WATER

Excellent water, still or sparkling, should taste fresh and clean. After you swallow, it should leave your mouth refreshed. It should be clear and free of sediment, with no aroma and no hint of a chemical taste such as chlorine. But the taste of excellent water isn't exactly no taste at all. Flatness—a lifeless taste—is a defect, often the result of very low mineral content.

Tap water shouldn't be brown, cloudy, or murky-looking. It shouldn't foam or have a discernible odor. Sudden changes in water's appearance, taste, or aroma suggest possible problems. Many hazards in water are invisible, tasteless, and odorless. Laboratory analysis is the only sure way to ferret them out. If you are concerned, contact your local water department or health department. They may test your tap water free of charge. If not, you might have to work your way up to your state's water-supply or health department.

Such agencies often test only for bacteria, not for toxic substances. In that case, consider a commercial laboratory. One such lab is the WaterTest Corp. (P.O. Box 6360, 33 S. Commercial St., Manchester, NH 03108; telephone 800-H2O-TEST.) This company charges from $99.95 to $150, depending on how many aspects of the water you want tested. The lower-priced test covers 25 metals and minerals.

Boiling tap water for 20 minutes is the standard remedy for bacterial contamination. To improve taste, try refrigerating your water. Heavy chlorine tastes and odors dissipate if water is kept for several hours in an uncovered pitcher or churned by a blender or mixer for a few minutes. A simple faucet aerator may make flat-tasting water more palatable.

Home water-treatment systems are also available. They include activated carbon filters, some of which attach directly to the faucet or hook into the cold-water line under a sink. A carbon filter can improve the taste and odor of water. It can also remove many organic chemicals, but it won't take out toxic metals or excessive minerals. However, you must replace the filter cartridges periodically, lest you actually add pollutants to your water.

Other home-treatment systems use reverse osmosis, ion-exchange resins, or distillation to soften water by removing minerals. Ion-exchange systems usually replace minerals with sodium, undesirable for those who want to restrict their sodium intake.

Wisdom in the Kitchen

CLEANSERS, SCOURING

Most scouring powders contain silica, a quartz dust so hard it can scratch glass, plastic, and enamel surfaces. Many new "soft" liquid cleansers contain milder abrasives. But even the softest can do some damage. Regular use of any abrasive scouring product will gradually scratch the shiny surfaces of sinks, bathtubs, porcelain enamel, and kitchen appliances. Some other tips:

• Whatever product you use, remember that the effects of abrasion are cumulative. You might not scuff up a tub right away, but light scrubbing over a long period of time will eventually ruin the finish. Don't apply scourers with a heavy hand and a hard pad. Use a sponge or a soft cloth at first, and use a rougher applicator only if you can't get the cleaning effect you want.

• Cleaning products that contain chlorine bleach or acid should not be mixed with other cleansers. Chlorine bleach reacts with ammonia or acid to produce dangerous gases.

• When you are cleaning, take off jewelry or wear rubber gloves. Scouring cleansers can dull the polish on a ring and scratch soft gems such as pearls and opals. The chlorine bleach in some products can discolor silver.

COFFEE MAKERS

Connoisseurs wouldn't consider preparing coffee in anything but a nonelectric, glass drip maker. But an automated coffee maker, most commonly an electric drip pot, can make a quite satisfactory brew. In shopping for an electric coffee maker, consider these key factors:

Water reservoir. It should be easy to fill. Avoid a reservoir with a small opening or an obstruction that would make you take careful aim with the water. The reservoir should be removable, and easy to clean, especially important if you don't make coffee every day.

Coffee basket. A one-piece basket is handier than a multipiece one, which must be assembled whenever you brew. Prefer a basket that slides into the brewing unit to one resting on the coffee carafe, which must be removed before you pour.

Filter. Disposable paper filters, shaped like a cupcake wrapper or a cone, cost up to about a nickel apiece. There are also reusable mesh filters, including gold ones. A gold filter costs about $25, but it can provide a full-flavored brew. (It may, however, allow some coffee sediment through and it takes extra attention to clean.)

Carafe. A carafe shouldn't have to be turned almost upside down to be emptied. It's helpful if the carafe is marked off in cups and has a knuckle-guard to prevent burns. An insulated carafe can keep coffee drinkably warm for hours on your table.

Automatic drip-stop. That feature keeps the last few drops in the coffee basket from dripping onto the hot plate when you remove the carafe.

Pause-to-pour control. That lets you pour a cup of coffee before the machine has finished brewing. That cup is likely to be quite strong, and later cups may turn out too weak if too many early cups are poured.

Brew-strength control. That level regulates how much of the grounds get soaked with water, handy if you don't like coffee particularly dark.

Clock. If you fill the reservoir and basket the night before, a built-in clock timer lets you have your coffee literally "first thing in the morning." But there's a trade-off for that convenience: Ground coffee that sits in the basket overnight loses a certain amount of freshness.

No matter which coffee maker you choose, you'll probably have to experiment with coffee brands and grinds to brew that "perfect" cup. If any coffee maker, old or new, isn't producing satisfactory coffee, try a finer grind, a better grade, or a darker roast. Make sure the coffee is fresh. You might also try a more porous filter; very dense filters can reduce flavor.

COOKWARE: A BASIC COLLECTION

Half a dozen pieces of well-designed cookware will see you through most recipes. There is no practical reason to buy cookware in a matching set. If, for example, you buy a set with metal handles so you can use the skillet for broiling, you are stuck with several hot-handled saucepans. Here's a list of the basic rangetop cookware every kitchen should have:

Saucepans. You'll need at least two—a two-quart and a three-quart size—with lids and comfortable, plastic handles. Look for sturdy stainless-steel saucepans with copper or aluminum embedded in the bottom. A nonstick-coated saucepan is optional, but handy for hard-to-clean oatmeal, puddings, or sticky sauces.

Fry pans. You'll need a 10-inch skillet that heats very evenly (a laminate of copper or aluminum with stainless steel) and a 7- to 10-inch "gourmet" pan with a nonstick coating. As a rule, skillets have steep sides and gourmet, sauté, or omelette pans have shallow, curved sides. Steep-sided pans usually hold more and are good for frying or cooking food items in liquid. A gourmet pan's sloped sides make it easier to slide in a spatula when turning an omelette or fried eggs.

Like a saucepan, the skillet should be made of stainless steel with an aluminum or copper bottom. Cast aluminum is an acceptable substitute, but you can't wash a pan with an anodized-aluminum surface in a dishwasher.

Dutch oven. A Dutch oven is used for baking, braising, and "broasting"—browning the meat on top of the stove before transferring it to the oven to bake. A Dutch oven should be made of thick aluminum or cast iron to hold the heat. The handles should be metal, to withstand even a hot oven.

Stockpot. Stockpots rely on liquid in the pot to

distribute heat; they have a relatively narrow bottom and high sides. You can save money by buying a pot made from plain aluminum, stainless steel, or porcelain-coated steel. If you choose aluminum, make sure the bottom is thick enough to resist dents.

Some options. You may want to add a double boiler for delicate sauces, a large inexpensive pot for boiling pasta and corn, and a cast-iron skillet.

Taking care of cookware. To prolong the life of your pans, always match the pan size to the burner; use the lowest possible heat for whatever dish you are cooking. If you overheat a metal pan, don't plunge it into cold water and don't heat a pan you just took from the freezer. Don't chop or slice anything in a pan. Scratches can mar a pan's looks and make it difficult to clean. Always use plastic or wooden utensils with nonstick pans. When cleaning, soak before you scrub. And never scour pans using stainless steel with abrasive cleansers.

DISHWASHERS

The more expensive a dishwasher, the more buttons and cycles. As you go down a manufacturer's line, you get progressively fewer cycles and control options. Basic models may have only one cycle, a dial, and a switch for no-heat drying. But even a basic machine should wash dishes well enough, particularly if you rinse dishes under a tap before stowing them in the machine.

Running a dishwasher takes about one-half to one kilowatt-hour of electricity per cycle—about 5 to 9 cents at the national average electricity rate of 8.2 cents per kwh. That comes to less than $30 a year, assuming one wash per day.

Most of a dishwasher's running costs are not for electricity, but for heating its water. If you turn down your water heater's output temperature from 140°F to 120°, you can save about $35 a year (with an electric heater) or $12 (with gas). And you get those savings without using any water at all. They're a reduction in the heat lost from your pipes and the water heater itself.

Unfortunately, you may not get by with 120° water unless the dishwasher has a built-in booster heater. Dishwashers need 140° water to liquefy some fatty soils and to dissolve detergent completely.

Safety. Dishwashers generally have safety mechanisms built-in. An interlock turns the machine off when you open the door. There is also a sensor to guard against an overfill if the timer sticks or is tampered with in the middle of a cycle.

Don't try to clean a filter or retrieve items from the bottom of a dishwasher's tub until the heating element under the lower rack has had a chance to cool off. Children should stay clear of a running machine: Door vents may emit hot steam.

Construction. A stainless-steel interior is absolute protection against scratches and chips that can expose metal to corrosion. A porcelain coating resists scratches very well, but it can be chipped if you drop something.

Plastic-tub machines and some with a porcelain tub use a plastic panel for the door's inner surface. That's a good material for an area otherwise likely to be damaged by dropped items.

DISHWASHER DETERGENTS

You can save money on detergent if you have a good dishwasher and soft water, particularly if you rinse dishes before washing them. If that's your situation, buy the cheapest dishwasher detergent you can find—a brand name on sale can cost less than a supermarket brand. However, with hard water, a so-so machine, or other dishwashing problems, it's best to use the most effective detergent possible.

Powdered detergents have been around a long time. They aren't perfect: They can cake in the box or in a dishwasher's dispenser cup. They may also leave gritty, undissolved deposits on dishes and glassware, especially if you pour in the detergent and don't start the dishwasher immediately.

Liquid dishwasher detergents, relatively new to the marketplace, are supposed to solve the problems of the powdered products. These "liquids" are actually gels containing a lot of fine, powdered clay and other suspended solids. They're thick enough to stay put in the dispenser cup when you close the dishwasher door. Otherwise, they resemble powders quite closely in makeup. In troublesome situations, the best performer is still apt to be a powder.

In general, a name-brand product usually cleans better than a store brand and is less likely to leave glass plates and tumblers cloudy or spotted. Liquids aren't as good as the best powders at keeping glasses free of water spots and food debris. Liquids can also leave an unsightly film on glasses instead of the powders' annoying grit.

It's best to hand-wash good china, particularly if the decoration is applied over the glaze. Overglazes are applied after the main glaze and are less durable. The same is true of gilding and other metallic decorations.

FREEZERS

A well-stocked freezer can be a great convenience, especially for a large family. But it can also cause you to waste money. Without proper wrapping and rotation of your stock, you can ruin a lot of food—too long a stay in the freezer can make the tastiest of foods inedible.

Managing your freezer. It doesn't take much to manage a freezer wisely:

• When starting up a freezer, leave a freezer thermometer in the center of the empty compartment for at least a day to make sure the freezer is working properly. If need be, adjust the thermostat for a reading at or near 0°F. Recheck the temperature winter and summer, resetting the thermostat as necessary.

• To learn which foods freeze best, check the freezer's manual. Or send for the U.S. Dept. of Agriculture's booklet 142M, "Home Freezing of Fruits and Vegetables" (Consumer Information Center [P], P.O. Box 100, Pueblo, CO 81002). Nutritionally, meat, fish, poultry, and eggs are the same frozen or fresh. Fruits and vegetables lose vitamins if they're not handled properly before freezing.

• Without proper wrapping, frozen food suffers "freezer burn" or dehydration. Wrap food securely. Use vapor-proof plastic wrap, aluminum foil, or plastic containers with snap-on lids. Don't rely on waxed paper, butcher's paper, regular polyethylene plastic wrap, or cardboard ice cream cartons. Rewrap all supermarket-packaged meat. Expel whatever air you can from a package before sealing it.

Use freezer tape, rubber bands, twist ties, or string to seal the wrapping.

• Label packages with their contents, serving size, and (to help you use up food promptly) the date of freezing. To ensure that no foods stay frozen too long, try to balance the flow of food into the freezer with the flow out. Move the oldest packages to the top or front.

• Thaw food in the refrigerator. If you must speed the process, run lukewarm water over the package or use the defrost setting on your microwave oven. Never refreeze thawed food.

• Defrost the freezer when the frozen-food supply is low. Transfer the remaining food to your refrigerator's freezer or the refrigerator itself. (Failing that, wrap the food in layers of newspapers.) Use pans of hot water and a small fan to speed defrosting. Never use a knife, ice pick, or other sharp object to loosen ice and frost.

GARBAGE BAGS

There are "garbage" bags and "trash" bags, "kitchen" bags and "wastebasket" bags, "lawn" bags and "leaf" bags. The name, along with some fine print on the package, is supposed to help you pick the right-size bag for your needs. But bags of the same nominal type and size often don't have identical capacities. Some manufacturers measure a bag's capacity when it's filled to the brim; others measure with the bag closed. There are no industry-wide standards, so some "26 gallon" bags may not fit a 26-gallon can.

The thickness of a bag's plastic or the number of plies, as given on the label, aren't good guides to quality, either. A bag that's 2 mils (0.002 inch) thick may be weaker than a 1.3-mil bag. Nor are multiple-ply bags necessarily stronger than single-ply ones.

That being so, it pays to buy the cheapest bags that meet your needs most of the time. When you need extra strength for an occasional heavy load, try double-bagging—slipping one bag inside the other.

MICROWAVE COOKWARE

Once you start using a microwave oven, you'll find yourself changing old habits. One of them is what you cook in. You'll make hot chocolate in the same cup you drink from. You'll heat dinner right on your plate. Stainless-steel cookware will be left hanging on the wall. Metal reflects microwave energy—use a metal pot in a microwave oven and you'll get either a cold meal or a damaged oven.

Many common kitchen items are fine for microwave cooking. Bacon cooks well in paper towels. You can defrost foods right in their plastic freezer containers (with the cover off), so long as you're careful not to heat the food enough to melt the plastic. You can even heat food in straw serving baskets.

Most ceramic or glass casseroles and baking dishes for use in a regular oven also work in a microwave oven. Such utensils cost a lot less than many dishes designed for microwave use. An "old fashioned" glass dish may suit your needs just fine. Still, if you use a microwave a lot, you may want some cookware made specifically for the purpose.

A utensil's shape affects its performance in a microwave oven. Round pans are superior for casseroles and meat loaf; in rectangular ones, food in the corners tends to overcook. Food also cooks more evenly when spread out in a shallow pan. Most glass and ceramic microwave utensils can also be used in a regular oven, if it's no hotter than 375° to 400°F. Few, if any, microwave pots and pans are usable on a range top. Plastic microwave utensils may also serve in a regular oven, but they may give off an unpleasant odor.

Clever design gives many microwave utensils versatility. Casserole lids, for example, may be usable as cooking vessels. Some open roasting racks double as baking trays. Others come with a trivet to use when roasting and remove when baking. A few racks come with a cover to help keep food from drying out and spattering during cooking.

Food browns better in a microwave oven when you use a special browning dish, but still not as appetizingly as when cooked the traditional way. Grilled cheese sandwiches turn out pale and unevenly cooked—the cheese melts before the bread shows much color. If you don't like microwaved roasts, you don't need a special roasting rack. Microwave ovens don't bake well, so baking utensils aren't essential.

To see if one of your nonmetal dishes or utensils is usable in a microwave, set the oven for High and put the dish inside for about eight minutes. If the dish stays fairly cool to the touch, it's probably all right for microwave use. But don't use good china or dishes with a decorative metal trim in a microwave. Be careful of pottery, which may have metal in the glaze or impurities in the clay.

MICROWAVE OVENS

A microwave oven can't substitute fully for a regular kitchen oven. It can't, by itself, produce a roast turkey with crispy skin, or a pair of cake layers that do justice to the baker.

True, some microwave ovens have a browning element. Others claim to offer the virtues of a regular oven, too. There's even a combination microwave oven/toaster oven/broiler. But unless you're assembling a family of appliances from scratch, chances are you will find a microwave oven handy mainly for heating, reheating, thawing, and cooking such things as baked potatoes, vegetables, and bacon.

Size. Microwave ovens are often classified by capacity. Subcompacts have an interior space of 0.5 cubic feet (cu. ft.) or less. Compacts run 0.6 to 0.7 cu. ft.; midsize models, up to 1.0 cu. ft.; and full-size ovens, larger than 1.0 cu. ft. But there's no standardization. Look for outer dimensions that fit your available space, and an interior big enough to accommodate the cookware you'll use.

Speed. A "magnetron" generates a microwave oven's cooking rays. In most full-size ovens, it produces about 700 watts of power for cooking. High power speeds up defrosting. You can also accelerate the roasting of a turkey or other large items by cooking it partially in a microwave oven, then switching to a regular oven to finish up and crisp the skin.

A subcompact or compact oven produces between 200 and 500 watts of power and is too small for a turkey. The average small oven takes about 30 percent longer than a full-size model to do the same job. That may mean only a minute, more or less, in added cooking time for a small item; one baked potato, for instance. But for a larger dish like a casserole, the difference would be 10 or 15 minutes.

Microwave cooking instructions tend to be approximations: You will probably find it necessary to adjust the recommended cooking times in recipes or on food packages.

Features. A deluxe microwave oven offers complex automated controls and features you may not really need or want. Give serious thought to buying a less-deluxe unit. Some options:

• *Controls.* Exact timing is important in microwave cookery, so electronic controls are a convenience. They let you set even the shortest cooking time exactly. Dial-type mechanical timers are less precise, and are generally found on less-expensive ovens.

• *Power levels.* Five power-level settings are enough for any task, though some units offer ten or more.

• *Sensors and probes.* On some deluxe models, a sensor detects moisture escaping from covered food and automatically "figures" the necessary power level and cooking time. Microwave ovens excel at cooking vegetables. An automatic sensor simplifies that job, but with a little experience, you'll be able to set the oven by hand expertly without it.

A probe functions somewhat like a meat thermometer. It's most useful for bulky foods like casseroles.

• *Programming.* Some microwave ovens come pre-programmed with a memory for cooking common foods. You just punch in the weight and type of food, and the machine does the rest. You can also program and store instructions of your own for special dishes.

• *Turntable.* Ovens with rotating turntables don't necessarily make food cook more evenly; they do make cooking more predictable. But a turntable reduces an oven's capacity. If you want a microwave mainly for reheating food or auxiliary cooking, you can get by without a turntable.

OIL AND FAT FOR COOKING

Oil is simply fat that's liquid at room temperature. Oil and fat are the most concentrated sources of energy in the human diet. They also carry the vitamins A, D, E, and K, and they're the chief source of an essential fatty acid, linoleic acid.

But fat that isn't expended as body heat and energy is easily converted to body fat, so a high-fat diet can lead to obesity. Furthermore, consumption of "saturated" fat can help elevate blood cholesterol levels, a risk factor for heart attacks. It makes sense, then, to cut some fat from your diet—especially the saturated kind.

Fat and oil from vegetable sources contain fewer saturated and more polyunsaturated fats than animal fats do. Liquid oil is usually less saturated than solid fat.

Saturated fat tends to increase the blood's cholesterol level. But polyunsaturated fat tends to lower that level; monounsaturated fat (the kind in olive oil) may have a similar effect. Accordingly, people with elevated cholesterol are often advised to eat less saturated fat and more of polyunsaturated fat.

Coconut oil and palm oil, common in many supermarket foods (particularly crackers and cookies), are high in saturated fat. Other vegetable oils are relatively low. But there are some differences. Low erucic acid rapeseed oil (Canola) is the least saturated—about 6 percent. Safflower and sunflower oil are next (about 10 percent saturated). Soy and corn oil are a little more so (about 14 percent); peanut oil is the most saturated (about 20 percent) of common vegetable oils. For comparison: Butterfat is about 60 percent saturated.

Most vegetable oil is naturally high in polyunsaturates (about 50 to 80 percent). Unlike the other oils, olive oil and canola oil are mostly monounsaturated fat. They're not high in saturated fat, but not high in polyunsaturates either.

Shortening made from vegetable oil is relatively high in saturated fat because it has been solidified by "hydrogenation," which saturates oil to some extent. (Hydrogenation also helps retard spoilage. Even certain liquid oils, such as soybean oil, are routinely hydrogenated a bit to make them keep longer.) All-vegetable-oil shortening has a saturation of between 25 and 30 percent.

Shortening that contains meat fat is even more saturated—above 40 percent. And meat fat contains cholesterol in significant amounts. Vegetable fats and oils contain none.

A tip on deep frying. Many people discard cooking oil after each session of deep frying. High-quality oil can be reused if it's filtered through cheesecloth or a fine sieve to remove burned food particles. Infuse it, by a quarter to a third, with fresh oil at each new use, to minimize any tendency for it to begin smoking at an ever lower temperature.

OVEN CLEANERS

If you're facing cleanup chores in your oven, have a care with oven cleaners that contain lye (sodium hydroxide). Corrosively alkaline, lye is one of the most dangerous substances sold for household use.

Before using a cleaner containing lye, protect yourself by wearing a long-sleeved shirt and rubber gloves. If you use an aerosol, wear a paper dust mask and goggles. Cover nearby floors, counters, and other surfaces with newspaper.

Packaging affects the convenience and safety of oven cleaners. *Pads* don't create airborne particles of lye and are handy for quick spot cleaning. *Aerosols* are easy to apply but are too easy to get on gaskets, heating elements, and sometimes on your face. A broad, concave button on the aerosol, rather than a small button, makes it harder to misdirect the spray. An *adjustable pump spray* can be a real annoyance. The adjustable nozzle produces anything from a stream to a misty, broad spray. The stream doesn't cover much and splatters; it's also diffuse and too easy to inhale. *Brush-on jelly* is tedious to use and almost impossible to keep from spattering.

There *is* a brighter side, however. There's at least one brand of oven cleaner on the market, made without lye, that isn't hazardous. This type of cleaner won't be quite as effective as some lye cleaners, but a second application should finish up even demanding jobs nicely.

Even if you don't have a self-cleaning oven or one with a continuous-clean finish (on which, incidentally, you can't use an oven cleaner), you aren't sentenced to the hard labor of oven cleaning. An oven in continual use can reach a steady state at which grime burns off at the same rate it accumulates. Serious spills, such as overflow from a cake pan, can be scraped up after the oven cools. A little dirt in the oven never hurt anybody. A little oven cleaner might.

OVEN THERMOMETERS

If recipes have been taking longer or shorter to cook than they ought, consider buying an oven thermometer. That will let you check the accuracy of your oven's thermostat.

To take a measure, put the thermometer at the center of the oven. Set the oven for the temperature you use most often and let it heat at least 15 minutes. Then take several readings at 10- to 15-minute intervals and average the results. Compare the average with the thermostat setting.

If the oven's temperature is incorrect, you can mark the thermostat dial to remind yourself to set the oven higher or lower than the dial indicates. Alternatively, call a technician to recalibrate the oven—or do it yourself, if the oven's instructions tell you how.

If you often cook on both top and bottom shelves of the oven, you may want to check temperatures in both places. You're apt to find a considerable difference between the two, but there's not much to do about it, except to change cooking times to compensate for the difference.

Mercury thermometer. Oven thermometers come in dial and mercury-in-glass formats. A mercury model is generally very accurate, but the mercury can be hazardous if you break the thermometer. A metal-encased mercury thermometer should be hard to break, even if dropped, but it could pose a special hazard. If left in the oven during a self-cleaning cycle, the thermometer is likely to burst, releasing highly toxic mercury vapor.

Should a mercury thermometer ever break, sweep the mercury into a dustpan, if possible, or pick up as much as you can with an eyedropper. Do not use a vacuum cleaner—it will vaporize the mercury and spread it through the room air. Place collected mercury in a jar or bottle with a lid, and throw it away. Air the room thoroughly.

RANGES

Microwave ovens now do some of a regular oven's tasks. But for baking and broiling, you really need an ordinary oven, too. Most people buy a 30-inch-wide freestanding range. Some buying considerations:

Cooktops. Some people prefer a cooktop with gas burners, which allows more precise control over heat than an electric one. Control is especially useful for simmering delicate sauces or for quick bursts of high heat in wok cookery. Ranges with knobs that turn nearly a half circle allow finer adjustments than those that rotate only ninety degrees.

Oven cleaning. A self-cleaning oven has a high-heat setting that reduces food soil to an ashy residue in a few hours. (The oven door locks automatically during the cleaning cycle.) Self-cleaning ovens are usually electric, rather than gas, models. A built-in vent carries away oven vapors during cooking and self-cleaning. The vent creates an additional cleaning chore by soiling either the backguard or the cooktop, depending on which way the vent faces. In some ranges, the vent is not guarded, making it easy to drop something into the vent. Retrieving the object could require major disassembly.

A continuous-cleaning oven has a special coating that supposedly helps dirt burn off as it accumulates. The process, however, isn't remarkably effective. You can't clean a continuous-clean oven by hand; the surface won't tolerate it.

Cooktop cleaning. Some design details make it easier to hand-clean a cooktop. Look for:

- Removable drip pans.
- Controls on a vertical surface, which won't get dirty quite so fast as horizontal controls.
- Seamless curves at corners and where the backguard meets the cooktop.
- A hinged cooktop, for easy access to the space under the top burners or heating elements.
- Plain trim. Avoid chrome; it demands continual wiping to keep it spotless, and it catches grease and dirt.
- Porcelain-finished drip bowls under heating elements and burners. Shiny metal bowls soon lose their shine, become scratched when cleaned, and may rust.

Reliability. In general, a gas range is more complicated and so is less reliable in the long run than an electric. Self-cleaning ranges of either type are less reliable than manual-clean models.

REFRIGERATOR/FREEZERS

When you're buying a refrigerator, what do you look for? The basic choice for most people is a side-by-side or a top-freezer model. A side-by-side model has its advantages: When open, its doors need about a foot less clearance in front than a top-freezer model, useful in a crowded kitchen. You can store quick-turnover items in the middle of each compartment, so you can get to them without stretching or stooping. And the compartments' tall, thin shape makes it easy to find stray food items. In the refrigerator of a top freezer, nothing can be stored at eye level.

However, a side-by-side refrigerator/freezer costs more to buy than a top-freezer unit, and it will use slightly more electricity, even after adjusting for capacity differences. Side-by-sides also tend to need repairs more often than top freezers.

Main shelves. Most shelves in the main compartment should be adjustable. A side-by-side model has at least four full-width shelves. Many top-freezer units have half-width shelves that provide extra flexibility—but more chances to knock things over unless the shelves are properly aligned.

Freezer. Main freezer shelving is usually plastic or wire—fixed in most side-by-sides, adjustable in most top-freezers. Side-by-side models have a utility bin or basket under the bottom shelf. Some models have a handy juice-can dispenser in the freezer door. An ice maker, although handy, takes up a lot of freezer space.

Door. Some side-by-sides have three doors. The third door conceals the ice maker and one small shelf. That lets you get ice without opening the main freezer door and helps to hold the freezer at a steady temperature. All doors should have detents to hold them open and stops to keep them from hitting an adjacent cabinet.

Door shelves. Adjustable shelves are handy. Extra-deep shelves are good for holding six-packs or gallon milk containers. Some shelves are like bins—you can use them to tote their contents to a kitchen counter. Retainers should keep a door shelf's contents from toppling out when you open the door quickly. There should be at least one door compartment for butter or margarine. Its cover should stay up when raised, to let you get at the contents with one hand.

Handles. Before you buy, try handles for comfort and clearance for your knuckles.

Cleaning. Bottom-mounted condenser coils are

easier to clean than back-mounted coils, but they may need cleaning every three months or so—they tend to collect dust. Use a condenser-coil cleaning brush and a vacuum cleaner's crevice tool. Back-mounted coils don't collect as much dust, but you have to move the refrigerator to get at them. Refrigerator interiors are easiest to clean if they have a seamless liner.

★ 8 ★

Keeping Warm,
Keeping Cool

AIR CONDITIONERS

The first step in choosing a room air conditioner is to determine the cooling capacity you need. An undersize air conditioner won't cool adequately; an oversize unit may cycle off before it can dehumidfy your room.

The smallest room air conditioners have a cooling capacity of about 4,000 British thermal units (Btu) per hour; the largest, about 20,000 Btu per hour. It takes about 7,500 to 8,500 Btu per hour to cool one large room in the Southeast or a couple of rooms in the Northeast. Use the worksheet on pages 103–105 to determine which size meets your needs.

You should also look for a unit that is thrifty with electricity. Every new air conditioner carries a tag that lists its Energy Efficiency Ratio, or EER. The higher the EER, the less the unit will cost to run. Some models have an "energy saver" setting that shuts off the fan when the compressor cycles off. However, the feature isn't likely to save much electricity—it's the compressor, not the fan, that uses most of an air conditioner's power. The setting may also make a room feel slightly stuffy.

Brownouts. In very hot weather, power companies often lower the line voltage. It's then best to set an air conditioner's thermostat at maximum cooling, to save strain on the compressor. Alternatively, turn the thermostat to a warmer setting to give the air conditioner a longer rest between cycles.

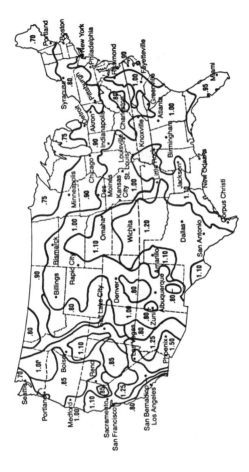

HOW POWERFUL AN AIR CONDITIONER DO YOU NEED?

This worksheet, adapted from one published by the Association of Home Appliance Manufacturers, can help you estimate how much cooling capacity you need. *Note:* Consider rooms connected by a permanently open door or archway more than 5 feet wide as one large room. If the air conditioner will be used only at night, use the factors given in parentheses to calculate the cooling load.

1. *Heat gain through doors.* Multiply the total width of all continually open doors in the room by the factor given. Consider rooms connected by a door or archway more than 5 ft. wide as one large space.

_____ ft × 300(200) = _____

2. *Sun through windows.* Multiply window area by the applicable factor. Multiply factor by 0.5 for any window with glass block; multiply factor by 0.8 for double glass or storm window. Enter only the largest number you calculate for the room. Disregard this item if air conditioner will be used only for night cooling.

Window facing	No shades		Inside shades		Outside awnings	
Northeast	sq. ft. × 60	or	25	or	20 =	
East	sq. ft. × 80	or	40	or	25 =	
Southeast	sq. ft. × 75	or	30	or	20 =	
South	sq. ft. × 75	or	35	or	20 =	
Southwest	sq. ft. × 110	or	45	or	30 =	Enter only
West	sq. ft. × 150	or	65	or	45 =	largest
Northwest	sq. ft. × 120	or	50	or	35 =	factor
North	sq. ft. × 0	or	0	or	0 =	

(continued)

3. *Conduction through windows.* Multiply total area of all windows by the factor given (use 7 as the factor if the windows have double glass or glass block).

          _____sq. ft. × 14 = _____

4. *Heat gain from walls.* Multiply total length, in feet, of all walls by the appropriate factor. Consider walls shaded by adjacent structures but not by foliage as having north exposure. "Light" means an uninsulated frame wall or a masonry wall no more than 8 in. thick. "Heavy" means insulated frame or masonry more than 8 in. thick.

	Light	Heavy
Outside, facing north:	_____ft. × 30(30) or 20(20) = _____	
Other outside walls:	_____ft. × 60(60) or 30(30) = _____	
Inside walls:	_____ft. × 30(30) or 20(20) = _____	

5. *Heat gain through ceiling.* Locate the type of construction that most closely matches that of the room to be cooled. Multiply the total ceiling area by the appropriate factor. Enter only one figure at far right.

Uninsulated, no space above	_____sq. ft. × 19(5) = _____	
Uninsulated, attic above	_____sq. ft. × 12(7) = _____	
Insulated, no space above	_____sq. ft. × 8(3) = _____	Enter only
Insulated, attic above	_____sq. ft. × 5(4) = _____	one figure
Occupied space above	_____sq. ft. × 3(3) = _____	

6. *Heat gain through floor.* Multiply total floor area by the factor given. Disregard this item if the floor is directly on the ground or over a basement.

          _____sq. ft × 3 = _____

7. *SUBTOTAL.* Add lines 1 through 6. Enter the result here. _____

8. *Climate correction.* Multiply the figure on line 7 by the climate-correction factor for your locality. Find the factor from the map on page 102.

_____(subtotal from line 7) × _____(factor from map) = _____

9. *Heat from people.* Multiply the number of people who will occupy the room to be cooled by the factor given. Use a minimum of 2 people.

_____(number of people) × 600 = _____

10. *Heat from electrical equipment.* Determine the total wattage for lights and electrical equipment in the room to be cooled. Don't include the air conditioner itself. If the appliance nameplate doesn't list the wattage, multiply the amperage by the voltage for an approximation

_____(total wattage) × 3 = _____

11. *TOTAL COOLING LOAD.* Add lines 8, 9, and 10. Enter the sum here. This number tells you how many British thermal units (Btu) of heat build up in the room each hour. Therefore, you want to choose an air conditioner with a cooling capacity (Btu per hour) that will nearly match the heat buildup you've calculated. A difference of about 5 percent between the number you calculate and the air conditioner's capacity shouldn't be significant.

Installation and maintenance. Your first step will usually be to mount a support bracket on the windowsill to brace the unit; the bracket often includes a leveling provision to ensure a slight tilt toward the outside. With big air conditioners, a slide-out chassis is a convenience—you can mount the empty cabinet before sliding in the heavy part.

Most air conditioners come with expandable curtains to fill the space at their sides. Metal frames are stronger than plastic.

Check the filter every week or so and wash or vacuum it as needed. A clogged filter reduces an air conditioner's effectiveness. It's also a good idea to dust the coil fins occasionally, inside and out. Some manufacturers suggest that you oil the fan motor periodically. That's easiest on models with a slide-out chassis.

Buy early. Late spring is best, before summer heat waves deplete retailers' stocks and your choice becomes limited.

FURNACES

New developments in home heating units can cut your fuel bills substantially. Over a heating season, your present furnace may misdirect as much as half of the heat you've paid for. But modern, high-efficiency designs deliver nearly all the heat content of their fuel to your living spaces. Even a furnace costing $2,000 or more can pay itself off rather quickly.

A new, high-efficiency furnace isn't for everyone. Unless you live in a particularly cold area or have unusually high energy costs, it probably doesn't pay to discard a recent, functioning furnace for a high-efficiency model. But if your furnace is more than 15 years old, an investment in a new high-efficiency unit makes sense.

Efficiency. Combustion, or Steady-State, Efficiency (CE or SSE) is the percentage of a fuel's energy that's converted into usable heat when a furnace operates continuously. CE is what a technician tests when tuning your furnace. CE measures only operating (or on-time) losses, so it doesn't tell you much about overall fuel use (there are also losses when a furnace cycles off). A better measure is the Annual Fuel Utilization Efficiency (AFUE), the percentage of the fuel's energy converted to usable heat over a full year's operation. The AFUE takes into account both on-time and off-time losses; it provides a good basis for comparing furnaces. High-efficiency furnaces are available with an AFUE of 90 percent and above.

If you now own a 15-year-old furnace, its AFUE is probably about 55 percent (if gas-fueled) or about 60 percent (if oil). You can boost those figures—but only a bit—by modifying the furnace. We tell you how below.

Use the worksheet on page 108 to figure your possible fuel savings in replacing your present gas or oil furnace with a high-efficiency one. There's a sample set of figures (for a home with an annual gas use of 1,600 therms) to show how it's done. The worksheet can't be used if you plan to switch fuels.

Upgrading an existing furnace. To get more efficiency from an old but still-serviceable furnace, consider "derating"—using a smaller nozzle in an oil furnace is likely to boost the AFUE by about 5 percent. Have the derating done as part of your furnace's annual tune-up, which should include a nozzle replacement anyway. Derating a gas furnace is not as easy. If you install a smaller orifice, you'll also have to modify the flue to restrict the flow of air, which your local building code may not allow.

Replace the pilot light of a gas furnace with an electronic ignition system (perhaps $200 for hardware and labor). You should save about 5 percent on your annual gas bill.

If your oil furnace is fairly old, install a flame-retention burner. It may cost as much as $600 to install, but can save you 15 to 20 percent a year on fuel.

HEATERS, ELECTRIC

A portable electric heater can save you fuel money. On cool spring or·fall days, you can leave your furnace off and use the heater to heat just the area you're in. For spot-heating—that is, warming an area quickly—a radiant or radiant convection unit is the best choice. The reflector in a radiant heater beams the heat to objects in its path. Convection-only models spread heat more slowly.

For safety, keep flammables, combustibles, furniture, and curtains away from a heater. Make sure a radiant heater's element is free of dust balls, hair,

HEATING WORKSHEET

	Example	Your House
Amount of fuel used now		
1. Number of units of fuel (therms of gas or gallons of oil) used per year.	1,600	_____
2. If some of that fuel is used to produce hot water, put 0.8 here. If none of the fuel is used for hot water heating, put a 1 here.	× 0.8	_____
3. Multiply line 1 by line 2.	= 1,280	_____
Amount of fuel used by new furnace		
4. Copy the number on line 3 here.	× 1,280	_____
5. Write the AFUE of your present furnace here. If you don't know what it is, use 55 for gas or 60 for oil.	× 55	_____
6. Multiply line 4 by line 5.	= 70,400	_____
7. Write the AFUE of the new furnace here.	÷ 90	_____
8. Divide line 6 by line 7. The answer is the number of units of fuel that you'll have to buy to heat your home with the new furnace for a year.	= 782	_____
Annual saving in dollars		
9. Copy the number on line 3 here.	1,280	_____
10. Copy the number on line 8 here.	= 782	_____
11. Subtract line 10 from line 9. The answer is the number of units of fuel you can save with the new furnace.	= 498	_____
12. Write the most recent price you paid for a unit of fuel.	× $0.62	_____
13. Multiply line 11 by line 12. The answer is the number of dollars you might save per year with the new furnace.	= $309	_____

or other flammable material. Clean its reflector with a vacuum cleaner (unplug the heater first) to improve its efficiency. Keep any heater away from water. If it tips over near water, don't try to right it before disconnecting the power.

If you use an extension cord, be sure it can handle 1,500 watts or $12\frac{1}{2}$ amperes; don't use a common lamp-type extension cord. Try not to use a heater on the same circuit with another high-wattage appliance, such as a toaster oven. Regularly check the wall outlet and the heater's plug and cord for excessive heat; a hot outlet may need replacement. A heater cord gets warm naturally, so don't cover it or leave it coiled or knotted. If the heater has a compartment for cord storage, withdraw the cord fully during use. Unplug the heater when it's not in use.

SHOWER HEADS, LOW-FLOW

If you live in an area that's drought-prone or where water is expensive, you have a simple way to save. A low-flow shower head can cut the water you use in the shower by 50 percent or more. It should also reduce your water-heating bill, since most water used in bathing is heated.

Bathing accounts for about 30 percent of the water a typical family uses. If your family takes mostly showers, a low-flow shower head should reduce your water use by 15 percent or more.

Before you buy a low-flow shower head, you might want to try a cheaper alternative—a simple device called a flow restrictor. You should be able to pick one up at a hardware store for about $2. A flow restrictor resembles a washer; it slips easily into the threaded fitting of the shower head. It will save water but it may diminish the flow's intensity more than you like. Then again, so may some low-flow shower heads.

TANKLESS WATER HEATERS

Instantaneous (or "tankless") water heaters promise unending hot water and lower water-heating bills. The reality can be less rosy.

These devices produce hot water as needed, instead of letting gallons of heated water sit—and lose heat—in a tank.

The heart of the device is a finned copper tube with a gas burner underneath. When you turn a hot-water tap to anything above a moderate flow, the burner turns on, heating the water that passes through the tube. After 10 to 15 seconds or so, the water from the heater becomes hot. When the tap is turned off, the unit shuts down.

Instantaneous gas heaters come in various sizes. Small models are meant to heat water for just one sink tap. However, they won't deliver hot water at a low flow, an inconvenience when you just want some warm water to wash your hands. The largest heaters, for their part, can't deliver water both hot enough and in sufficient volume to replace a conventional hot-water system. The big models are generally able to heat water for a shower or clothes washer, but they're not big enough to do more than one of those tasks at the same time. It may also take longer to run a hot bath or fill a washing machine than you're used to. And a flow-reducing shower head is a virtual necessity. Scalds aren't likely, but they're possible if you rapidly turn the faucet almost but not quite off. With a heater at its hottest setting, that maneuver could increase the water temperature by about 20°F. The effect, however, is momentary.

A whole-house instantaneous water heater is a good alternative to a conventional gas-fired heater only if you have special needs: If you don't have room for a regular heater, for example, or if you are a shower addict who wants an endless, if somewhat low-volume, flow of hot water.

A tankless heater probably isn't as prone to mineral buildup as a tank-type heater, and might, therefore, outlast a conventional unit when working with water with a very high mineral content. For safety reasons, you can't install an instantaneous heater in a closed space, such as a closet, bedroom, or bathroom; these heaters need venting to the outside.

WOOD STOVES

A wood stove looks like a quick, easy, and relatively inexpensive way to lower heating bills. A modern wood stove (usually one with a catalytic combustor) burns cleaner than its predecessors and so contributes fewer pollutants to the air and less flammable creosote to the chimney. It burns more efficiently and so consumes less wood. Still, there are drawbacks.

For most people, a wood stove is fundamentally an auxiliary heater. A stove may cost much less to run than an electric heater, but it costs considerably more to buy and install, and it requires much more of your time and attention.

If you want a stove for its cheeriness as much as for its warmth, you might want to choose for price, installation dimensions, or a feature such as a window or an ash drawer. Be sure to check prospects for ease of loading. And give preference to high-efficiency models.

Be extremely careful about installation. Don't do the work yourself unless you're an accomplished do-it-yourselfer. Check your fire department or building inspector about local requirements for minimum clearances and heat-shielding materials. Don't cut corners or skimp on materials. If you have a professional handle the installation, hire the company with the best reputation, not necessarily the lowest price.

★ 9 ★

Carefree Washdays

CLOTHES DRYERS

In the market for a clothes dryer? You'll probably be happiest with one with a moisture sensor. A sensor directly samples the moisture of loads and shuts the machine off as soon as clothes are dry, avoiding wasteful overdrying. The alternative, the temperature-sensor, checks dampness indirectly: As the clothes dry, air leaving the drum gets progressively hotter until a thermostat shuts off the heat. The timer then advances until the heat goes on again. That sort of back-and-forth continues until the heating part of the cycle has ended.

A moisture sensor, usually found in full-featured models, adds anywhere from $25 to $40 to a dryer's price. In some major brands, however, even models lower in the line also feature a moisture sensor.

Permanent press. All fabrics—but especially permanent-press clothes—will wrinkle if left in a warm heap. It's best to remove a load from the machine as soon as it's dry. Since that's often not feasible, dryers have a tumble-without-heat phase at the end of any automatic cycle to reduce wrinkle problems.

When you set the machine for permanent-press, that cool-down is generally extended somewhat to cool the load to room temperature. A short cool-down period causes some dryers to leave the load too warm. With most models, however, you can set an extra tumble period of 15 to 150 minutes to follow the automatic or permanent-press cycle when you put the load in to dry.

Gas versus electric. A gas dryer handles clothes about as well as an electric model. However, it does so for less than one-third the cost per load (assuming fuel at national average rates: electricity at 7.9 cents per kilowatt-hour, gas at 61.7 cents per therm, which is about 100 cubic feet). Drying a 10-pound load at those rates would run about six cents a load with gas, more than three times that with electricity. That estimate includes the electricity for the gas dryer's motor and controls.

If natural gas is available to you, it's worth spending the $40 or so premium that a gas dryer commands over its electric counterpart. The difference in purchase price can easily be made up in running-cost savings in the first year of use. Be sure to order a gas dryer specifically for the sort of gas (natural, LP, or whatever) it will burn.

Venting. The water a clothes dryer extracts from clothes emerges as warm vapor that's generally vented outdoors, lest it condense in the laundry room. Depending on your installation requirements, a machine may have to be vented from the rear, side, or bottom. Check that a machine can be vented from the location you need.

FABRIC SOFTENERS

You wouldn't need a fabric softener at all if it weren't for synthetic detergents, which tend to leave clothes feeling scratchy. Regular soap has a softening effect, largely because it doesn't rinse out of textiles as thoroughly as detergents do. Fabric softeners work by coating fabric fibers, much as hair conditioners coat hair, leaving a thin layer of waxy or soapy substance that makes the fabric feel "soft." The coating also separates a napped fabric's fibers and stands them on end, making the laundry fluff up. After testing more than a dozen of each type, we've come up with the following hints:

• Fabric softeners tend to work better in hard water than in soft. It's best to use fabric softener in the rinse cycle, after the detergent has done its work, or in the dryer.

• Detergent/softener combinations present a problem: The chemicals used for softening tend to neutralize the chemicals used for cleaning. Manufacturers have tried to work around this problem in various ways, but the compromises seem to work only at some cost in both cleaning and softening.

• Static cling is caused by the tumbling action of a clothes dryer—electrical charges build up on the surface of synthetic fabrics. A thin coating of fabric softener disrupts the buildup.

• You'll get best results, particularly if wash is done in hard water, with softener-impregnated dryer sheets. But the sheets must be used with caution. They generally carry a warning to use low-heat settings for synthetics and blends (oily spots might appear at higher heat, or if there are only a few items in the load). Liquids can also cause spotting if they are poured directly onto clothes. The remedy for softener spots is to moisten the fabric, rub the spot with a bar of plain soap, and wash again.

LAUNDERING

When filling a clothes washer, you can save some bother, and some money on hot water, with a simple approach that still gives a clean wash. Sort out the obvious trouble items—greasy overalls and brand-new blue jeans. Then wash everything else together in warm or cold water. If clothes aren't heavily soiled, and your laundry needs freshening more than scouring, you'll probably lose nothing in cleaning. And you'll have spared yourself the traditional chore of sorting whites from colored items and cottons from synthetics, washing some items in hot water, bleaching some things, and so forth.

However, you may still want to do a special load now and then. To do a load that's all colorfast cottons, for instance, use a hot wash/cold rinse; if the dirt is really bad, first let the load soak a while. If you use bleach, use liquid chlorine bleach, which can whiten twice as well as oxygen ''all-fabric'' bleaches. But don't use chlorine bleach on wool, silk, mohair, or items that aren't colorfast.

LAUNDRY BLEACHES

There's more than one kind of bleach. Which is the best to use? Both chlorine and nonchlorine bleaches use an oxidizing agent (usually sodium hypochlorite or sodium perborate) that reacts with a detergent to help lift out a stain. Chlorine bleach whitens best, but all-fabric powdered bleach has the advantage of being safe with most fabrics and dyes, even over the long term. However, they're a lot more expensive to use than chlorine bleach, and aren't as good at whitening.

You can get extra whitening performance out of powdered all-fabric bleaches, if you prefer them. If you double the recommended dose, a good all-fabric bleach approaches chlorine bleach in whitening ability.

LAUNDRY DETERGENTS

A large number of detergents compete for your washday dollar. The differences among them, however, are fairly minor. The dirt dissolvers in synthetic detergents are soaplike molecules (surfactants) that emulsify oil and grease and the dirt they attract and hold, allowing them to be washed away. "Anionic" surfactants are used most widely. They are especially effective at cleaning clay and mud from cotton and other natural fibers. The hotter the water, the better they work. However, they don't work well in hard water, so they are often compounded with water-softening compounds such as phosphates.

"Nonionic" surfactants are much less sensitive to hard water. They're particularly effective at cleaning oil soil from polyester and other synthetics in cool wash temperatures. Many liquid detergents are based on surfactants of this type.

Anionic surfactants are high sudsing; nonionic surfactants, low sudsing. Suds matter in a front-loading washing machine, where an excess can overflow or interfere with washing. In a top-loading washer, the amount of suds has no connection with a detergent's cleaning power.

Phosphates in detergents help soften the water, disperse dirt, and emulsify greasy soil. Unfortunately, they also help transform lakes into swamps. Consequently, they have been banned in a number of places and are unavailable to about 30 percent of the population, mostly in states around the Great Lakes and Chesapeake Bay. Manufacturers often make a phosphate and a nonphosphate version of the same powder brand to sell in different regions.

Nonphosphate powders typically use washing soda and a few extra ingredients to make up for phosphates.

Liquid detergents are phosphate-free, but they contain enzymes, which make otherwise insoluble stains easy to wash away.

Most detergents contain colorless, water-soluble dyes known as fluorescent whiteners or optical brighteners. The dyes convert invisible ultraviolet light into visible light, which gives fabrics a "glow." The effect doesn't work under incandescent light, so garments washed in a detergent containing whiteners may look drab in household lighting.

Special "anti-redeposition" agents in many detergents keep dirt in suspension until it's rinsed away. Even the best of these agents can't cope with lots of dirt, so wash heavily soiled items separately.

Washing ability. Differences between the best and worst detergents aren't very noticeable. The scale is really from clean to cleanest rather than from dirty to clean.

Fabrics. Synthetics hold onto stains more tenaciously than cotton and other natural fibers. And detergents behave differently on polyester and nylon. Polyester attracts oil, for instance, while nylon resists it. Nylon, however, tends to pick up colors from other items in the wash. Switching detergents may help solve nagging laundering problems.

Safety. Heed warning labels. Detergent chemicals can irritate eyes, mucous membranes, or sensitive skin. Keep detergents out of the reach of young children. Avoid prolonged contact with products that are extremely alkaline or that contain enzymes.

Skin rashes caused by a laundry product are generally not serious, and they disappear quickly when the irritant is removed. If you suspect a laundry product of causing rashes or other such problems, stop using it and see if the symptoms subside.

STEAM IRONS

Before buying a feature-laden modern iron, consider what you iron. If you just touch up permanent press now and then, a plain steam iron may serve. Chances are, however, that ironing chores will be a bit easier if you get an iron with more features.

Three sorts of person should consider paying for an iron with extras—those who press everything from cotton to acetate; those who are as apt to press in wrinkles as press them out; and those who want a steam iron that shuts off automatically.

Here are some features to look for:

● *Spray and burst of steam.* A built-in spray wets a little patch in front of the iron; a burst of steam at the press of a button lets you set creases or smooth stubborn wrinkles. Both features are useful for dealing with the wrinkles that crop up in natural fibers.

● *Automatic shutoff.* The simplest design has a small light that shines steadily while the iron is on. If you leave the iron upright for about 15 minutes or in the ironing position for half a minute without moving it, the light flashes and the iron shuts off. Another design has three lights—an amber light that glows while the iron is plugged in, a red Wait light that comes on when the iron is heating or cooling, and a green Ready light that comes on when the iron reaches the selected temperature. Such irons shut off after 10 minutes upright or about 30 seconds without movement in the ironing position. There are other arrangements, too, all of which are likely to work exactly as claimed.

● *Temperature control.* Look for a clearly marked control on the front of the handle, where you can adjust it with one hand. A control under the handle is hard to see and takes two hands to adjust.

● *Control buttons.* Look for clearly marked controls that can be easily operated with one hand. The best steam/dry controls are on the front of the iron. Many irons have the button awkwardly placed on the side. The best spray/burst-of-steam controls don't interfere with each other.

● *Fabric guide.* If you don't iron a lot, look for a guide that gives temperature settings for a variety of fabrics.

● *Cord (while ironing).* Try the iron to see if the cord hits your wrist. In the best design, the cord projects off to the side. You can switch the cord from side to side on a few models.

● *Water gauge.* Look for a see-through plastic water chamber. Very dark plastic tanks are nearly impossible to see through, although they do hide unsightly mineral accumulations.

● *Button groove.* Look for a groove that extends

along the side of the soleplate. If there are only short notches, they may be shallow and ineffective.

• *Weight.* Balance is probably more important than actual weight. Before you buy, pick up the iron and pretend to use it. It should feel well balanced and comfortable.

• *Cordless irons.* These irons heat up in a separate base that's plugged into the electrical outlet. To keep the iron hot, a cordless iron has to be set into its base often. That can be a nuisance.

WASHING MACHINES

Just about any machine you buy will wash clothes satisfactorily. The differences these days are in features:

Controls. Dials and levers are perfectly adequate, cheaper to service, and often more versatile than the touch-pad controls common on more expensive models.

Wash cycle. In all automatic machines, this cycle consists of wash-spin-rinse-spin. Full-featured machines generally have at least three such cycles—for regular, permanent-press, and delicate fabrics. Some have an extra cycle for soak and prewash.

The permanent-press cycle is generally a few minutes shorter than the regular cycle. To keep wrinkles from setting, clothes are cooled down with a cold spray or cold rinse before the first spin cycle. The spin speed is also slower; clothes are thereby not compressed hard, but they are a bit wetter than a regular wash at the end of the cycle. The delicate cycle has slower agitation and spin than the regular wash cycle.

Speed control. A selector for wash and spin is often built into the cycle control. But sometimes you have to set speeds independently.

Water-level control. The less hot water you use, the cheaper the machine is to run. A level control lets you adjust the water to the size of the wash load, thereby saving water, detergent, and energy.

Temperature setting. Any machine can wash in hot, warm, or cold water. There's little reason to use the hot setting, except for the occasional wash that won't come clean otherwise. You can save about half of your water-heating cost by using a warm wash instead. Using a cold wash is the ultimate saving, and it's effective for a lot of home laundering.

Always use a cold rinse; warm water doesn't rinse any better.

Tub capacity. A large tub lets you do a few large loads rather than more small ones.

Additional cycles. A deluxe machine may offer *Soak/prewash,* for heavily soiled clothes, or *Extra rinse,* for two rinses instead of one. *Sequential* means you can let the extra cycle proceed automatically; otherwise, the machine stops before or afterward, and you set the next step yourself. An automatic *bleach dispenser* adds bleach to the wash cycle after water has filled the tub. A *softener dispenser* holds fabric softener and dispenses it during the rinse cycle.

Within a manufacturer's line, a number of models often share the main mechanical parts and so should perform similarly. If you buy a less-expensive washer, usually all you give up are presoak and extra-rinse cycles and automatic dispensers for bleach and fabric softener.